The Canadian Way

An Immigrant's Guide to Settling in Canada

The Canadian Way

An Immigrant's Guide to Settling in Canada

By
Jo Davenport

eBookstand Books
http://www.eBookstand.com
http://www.CyberRead.com

Published by
eBookstand Books
Division of CyberRead, Inc.
Houston, TX 77079
1954_3

Edited by Emma at: www.wordsru.com

Disclaimer:

The author does not claim to be a Registered Representative; however, she has successfully immigrated to Canada on her own. In the process, she has become extremely knowledgeable about immigration procedures, as well as the most efficient and successful process to follow in settling in Canada. This book shares what she has learned through personal experiences and her extensive research.

ISBN 1-58909-299-6

Printed in the United States of America

National Anthem

O CANADA

O Canada!
 Our home and native land!
True patriot love
 in all thy sons command.
With glowing hearts
 we see thee rise,
The True North
 strong and free!
From far and wide,
 O Canada,
We stand on guard
 for thee.
God keep our land
 glorious and free!
O Canada,
 we stand on guard for thee.
O Canada,
 we stand on guard for thee.

O Canada!
 Terre de nos aïeux,
Ton front est ceint
 de fleurons glorieux!
Car ton bras
 sait porter l'épée,
Il sait porter
 la croix!
Ton histoire
 est une épopée
Des plus
 brillants exploits.
Et ta valeur,
 de foi trempée,
Protègera nos foyers
 et nos droits,
Protègera nos foyers
 et nos droits.

ACKNOWLEDGMENTS

I appreciate **Debbie Hatt** for being my true friend, for reviewing my book, and encouraging me as I spent endless hours researching the information for this book.

Thanks to **Celeste MacDonald**, who is an English Teacher at Middleton Regional High School, for editing the first version of my book.

Thanks to **Patty Phillips**, graphic artist with PJ's Arts & Graphics in Kingston, Nova Scotia for helping me create the book cover page.

Thank you also to **Philippe Renault**, Professional travel photographer, Canada for allowing me to use one of his lovely pictures for my book cover. You will want to see his pictures at the following site:

http://www.picturescanada.com/picturescanada.html

Phillip Townsend, author of "Passport to Canada the Complete Guide to Living and Retiring in Nova Scotia". Thank you, Phillip, for helping promote my book and for sharing your own book with me. You can find Phillip's book at:

http://www.nsliving.info

INTRODUCTION

Chances are, if you've come across this book, you're interested in immigrating to Canada. But first you must know one thing; you must apply to become an immigrant of Canada. It is a process that requires careful planning in many aspects of your life and finances.

I became a permanent resident of Canada in January, 2003. I spent years researching the information for the basis of this book, as it was not all readily available. I have attempted to impart a great deal of information in as concise a manner as possible on many different topics dealing with the entire immigration process. The intention is to make the process a bit easier by giving you some tools to use before, during and as you settle in Canada.

This book covers many topics, including:

How to plan for your immigration to Canada
The immigration process
History of Canada
Financial and tax-related issues
Filing two tax returns – Canada & US
Dual citizenship

This book was written to be used as a reference guide as a companion to the interactive version that can be downloaded in order to access the many web links included in the text.

Download the eBook interactive Microsoft Word document at the following web link:

http://www.thecanadianway.info/worddoc.zip

While the links may work at the time of publishing, web sites change frequently, so I apologize in advance for any broken links due to web sites closing down or moving.

I hope you find the topics discussed in this book to be helpful as you immigrate to Canada. If you have any questions or comments about the book, please email me at: askjo@thecanadianway.info.

Table of Contents

5

About the Author

Jo was born in Kentucky, grew up in Virginia and lived in Atlanta, Georgia for almost 20 years prior to settling in Nova Scotia.

After working for many years, she decided to go back to university to complete a degree. She worked full-time and attended classes in the evening and weekends, graduating magna cum laude in 1997 with a BA degree from Oglethorpe University. She worked for many years as an Administrative Assistant/Executive Director in Atlanta, Georgia, including over 12 years with the Rotary Club of Atlanta.

In 2001, she decided to move to Nova Scotia, Canada, and began researching how to immigrate. She successfully became a permanent resident of Canada in January, 2003. She applied on her own without the assistance of a personal representative or an immigration lawyer and learned many valuable lessons in the process.

After becoming a permanent resident of Canada, she took an H&R Block tax course and worked for the company for one season, while taking an online course in Financial Planning. She has found both courses extremely helpful in learning about taxation, finances and Canada in general.

She has spent years researching immigration to Canada and would like to share what she has learned with others. This book is a product of her love for research, the do-it-yourself approach to learning, and her experience in immigrating to Canada from the US.

Email Address: askjo@thecanadianway.info

Website: http://www.thecanadianway.info

1
Why Live in Canada?

There are many reasons one would want to immigrate to another country. Some people get tired of the same old routine and need a change, others have family or partners in other nations, some land new jobs or are transferred with old jobs and still others come because they are refugees.

Canada prides itself on being a peaceful country and sends peacekeeping forces to other countries. In fact, the central landmark of the Parliament buildings in Ottawa is called the <u>Peace Tower</u>.[ii]

Canada is a country where diversity is welcomed, where tolerance is the norm; and where people of different colour, race, religion, gender and sexual orientation cohabit in peace and harmony. The **Charter of Rights and Freedoms** is taken seriously in Canada and all who live in Canada have the right to be treated equally under the law.[iii]

There are two official languages in Canada – **English and French**. Both languages are taught in school and government documents are printed in both languages. In the US, there is only one official language - English.

Canada is a Democratic country and is similar in many ways to the US. The UN has consistently ranked Canada as one of the best places to live for several years running. A survey is performed annually by the UN using the Human Development Index (HDI). The areas considered include: life expectancy, educational achievement, access to education, standard of living, GDP per capita, adult literacy, universal healthcare, as well as the allowance of citizens to retain dual citizenship. Canada ranked #4 in 2004, and #1 for 7 years prior to that.[iv] The US ranked #8.[v]

The landscape is beautiful with parks, wilderness areas and nature reserves. All the provinces offer different terrain and different ecosystems.

You will find Canadians to be warm, down-to-earth, genuine people with a respect for all people.

2
Tell Me about Canada

The year 1997 marked the 50th anniversary of Canadians becoming citizens of their own country and no longer being British subjects. Paul Martin, Sr. was the cabinet minister responsible for passing the first Citizenship Act on January 1, 1947. He visited a military cemetery in France at the end of World War II, and was moved by the allegiance of those who died in the war. He then went on to help Canada establish a separate identity as a tribute to those who died in battle.[vi]

Canada is the second largest country in the world with an area of 10 million square kilometers. Its population, however, is quite small at just over 30 million people (2001 Census). The majority of Canadians live in the southern parts of the country with the largest population in Ontario. The second largest population lives in Quebec and the third largest lives in British Columbia[vii]. Canada is bordered by three oceans - the Pacific, the Atlantic and the Arctic. The national capital is Ottawa in the province of Ontario.

Listed below are the 10 provinces and 3 territories in order of when each joined the Confederation. The Confederation was created on July 1, 1867 by the first four provinces listed:

July 1, 1867 - Ontario
July 1, 1867 - Nova Scotia
July 1, 1867 - Quebec
July 1, 1867 - New Brunswick
July 15, 1870 - Manitoba
July 15, 1870 - Northwest Territories
July 20, 1871 - British Columbia
July 1, 1873 - Prince Edward Island
June 13, 1898 - Yukon Territory
Sept 1, 1905 - Alberta
Sept 1, 1905 - Saskatchewan
March 31, 1949 - Newfoundland & Labrador
April 1, 1999 - Nunavut Territory

The Northern Territories - Northwest Territories, Yukon and Nunavut - represent a third of Canada's land mass. Many natural resources are found there including oil, natural gas, gold, lead and zinc. Although these areas are rich in natural resources, they are very remote to live or to work in.

The word "Canada" comes from a First Nations term for a village "kanata". The first inhabitants of Canada were the First Nations people and today you find three main groups of Aboriginal peoples in Canada – First Nations, Inuits and Metis.

There are three main industries in Canada: natural resources, manufacturing and services. Natural resources include fishing, forestry, agriculture, mining and energy. Manufacturing consists of automobiles, paper, technological equipment, food, clothing and many others. The largest international trading partner is the USA. The service industry consists of transportation, education, health care, construction, banking, communications and government. The majority of working Canadians are employed by the service industry.

Canada retains some British ties in that Her Majesty Queen Elizabeth II is the Queen of Canada and Canada's Head of State. The Queen's representative in Canada is the Governor General. In October 2005 the Governor General of Canada was Michaelle Jean (formerly Adrienne Clarkson)[viii].

There are three levels of Government in Canada: federal, provincial or territorial and municipal (local). Parliament also has three parts: the Queen, the House of Commons and the Senate. Canada is a democracy with a parliamentary system of government. Each province elects representatives to the House of Commons (called MPs). The Senate is chosen by the Prime Minister and is appointed by the Governor General. Members of the Senate are called Senators. The Prime Minister is the leader of the political party with the most elected members of Parliament in the House of Commons (as of October 2005 the Prime Minister of Canada was Paul Martin, Jr.).

Federal elections must be held within five years of the last election. Any Canadian citizen aged 18 years or older can run for election.

This is a short introduction to Canada, its history and its method of governance. Additional information can be found in the section "**A Look at Canada**"[ix].

Province	Capital	Region	2001 Census	Main Industries
Alberta	Edmonton	Prairies	2,974,807	Agriculture, forestry, tele-communications, oil/gas.
British Columbia	Victoria	West Coast	3,907,738	Forestry, mining, fisheries, agriculture, energy, transport.
Manitoba	Winnipeg	Prairies	1,119,583	Manufacturing, agriculture, hydroelectricity, mining.
New Brunswick	Fredericton	Atlantic	729,498	Manufacturing, forestry, mining, agriculture, fisheries, tourism.
Newfoundland & Labrador	St. John's	Atlantic	512,930	Energy, fisheries, mining, forestry, tourism.
Northwest Territories	Yellowknife	North	37,360	Mining, tourism, services.
Nova Scotia	Halifax	Atlantic	908,007	Manufacturing, agriculture, fisheries, mining, forestry, transportation, energy.
Nunavut	Iqaluit	North	26,745	Mining, resource development, tourism.
Ontario	Toronto	Central Canada	11,410,046	Manufacturing, agriculture, forestry, mining, services.
Prince Edward Island	Charlottetown	Atlantic	135,294	Agriculture, tourism, fishing, manufacturing.
Quebec	Quebec	Central Canada	7,237,479	Agriculture, manufacturing, energy, mining, forestry, transportation.
Saskatchewan	Regina	Prairies	978,933	Agriculture, services, mining.
Yukon	Whitehorse	North	28,674	Mining, tourism.
		TOTAL	**30,007,094**	

3
A Few Differences in Canada & USA

Differences	USA	Canada
Official Language(s)	English	English / French
Government Style http://users.eastlink.ca/~d hh/index_files/page0001. html	Democracy Republic President – Head of State and Government	Democracy Constitutional Monarchy Governor General – Head of State Prime Minister – Head of Government
Healthcare (See Chapter 22 & 23)	Individual Plans & Medicare	Universal Healthcare
Exchange Rate http://www.bankofcanada .ca/en/exchange.htm (See Chapter 37)	If 0.65 US	is $1 CAD, then the conversion is: 1 / 0.65 = 1.5385
Metric System http://www.onlineconvers ion.com/	Gallons Pounds Miles	Litres - Multiply litres by .22 to convert to gallons. Kilograms - Multiply # kilograms by 2.205 to convert to pounds. Kilometres - Multiply # kilometres by .6214 to convert to miles.
Crime and Punishment	Capital punishment reinstated 1976.	Capital punishment abolished in 1976.
Lottery Winnings	Taxable and paid out over 20 years unless you request a cash option.	Tax-free and paid out in a lump sum.
Words Used in Canada	Letter "Z".	Pronounced "Zed" in Canada. (Use British spellings).

4
Immigration Class Overview

The Canadian Immigration system underwent a major overhaul, which became effective June 28, 2002. The new immigration rules are detailed here.

To get started, go to the Citizenship and Immigration Canada (CIC) website located at: http://www.cic.gc.ca

Choose your preferred language on the main page and then click on the link that says "To Immigrate" in the left column under "Choose Canada". On this site you will see the immigration classes currently available. Choose the one that you feel you qualify for and download all the relevant applications, guides and instructions. Be sure to look at all the links on each page.

The main Immigration classes in 2005 are:

> **Skilled Worker**: http://www.cic.gc.ca/english/skilled/index.html
> **Business** - http://www.cic.gc.ca/english/business/index.html
> **Provincial Nominee**:
> http://www.cic.gc.ca/english/skilled/provnom/index.html
> **Family**: http://www.cic.gc.ca/english/sponsor/index.html
> **Quebec-Selected**: http://www.cic.gc.ca/english/skilled/quebec/index.html

You should read the following before you start:
http://www.cic.gc.ca/english/skilled/before-1.html

Note: US Citizens visiting Canada do not require a visa (limited to less than six months stay). To enter Canada you may show a birth certificate, but it is preferable to have a passport, especially since the events of September 11. (A passport may become mandatory in December, 2006).

Selecting a Guide to Download from the CIC website.

IF YOU WOULD LIKE TO SPONSOR:	USE THIS GUIDE:
A spouse or common-law partner **In Canada** class. (no right of appeal)	**IMM 5289** – Applying for permanent residence from Within Canada. (Spouse or Common-law partner In Canada Class)
A spouse or common-law partner or dependent child who lives **outside of Canada**.	**IMM 3900** – Sponsorship of a spouse, common-law or conjugal partner, or dependent child living outside of Canada.
A spouse or common-law partner and you want a right of appeal.	**IMM 3900** – Sponsorship of a spouse, common-law or conjugal partner, or dependent child living outside of Canada.
A spouse or common-law partner but you are not eligible to sponsor them.	**IMM 5291** – Applying for permanent residence from Within Canada – Humanitarian and Compassionate Cases.
A temporary residence permit holder who has not resolved their inadmissibility as it relates to matters other than legal immigration status.	**IMM 5291** – Applying for permanent residence from Within Canada – Humanitarian and Compassionate Cases.
Other family members: parents, grandparents, adopted children and other relatives.	**IMM 5196E** **IMM 3998E**

Note: It is important to check the CIC website regularly, as immigration rules and policies change frequently. Also, you can use the Google search engine to do a quick search for all the guides above, by simply typing in the IMM number.

5
Skilled Worker Class

http://www.cic.gc.ca/english/pdf/kits/guides/EG7.pdf
http://www.hrsdc.gc.ca/en/epb/lmd/fw/supperimm.shtml

Do you qualify?

http://www.cic.gc.ca/english/skilled/qual-1.html

- You must meet the minimum work experience requirements, prove that you have funds for settlement, and earn enough points in the self-assessment test.

Self-Assessment Test: (minimum of 67 points required)

http://www.cic.gc.ca/english/skilled/assess/index.html

Forms & Guides:

http://www.cic.gc.ca/english/applications/skilled.html

- Download the main Federal Skilled Worker guide from the website above. You may also want to look at some of the other documents on the same website.

Occupation List:

http://www.cic.gc.ca/english/skilled/qual-2-1.html

- Find the occupation on the list above that best describes your skills and experience, then go to the following page and type in the code you chose of the occupation you chose in the Quick Search box (bottom left corner of following website) to find a more detailed description of the occupation:

http://www23.hrdc-drhc.gc.ca/2001/e/groups/index.shtml

Note: The job description doesn't have to fit your skills exactly, but should represent your basic skills and experience over the last 10 years. You should choose the one job that you have the most experience in; however, you can make note of other skills you have by attaching a letter with your application. The more skills you have, the better. This will help prove to CIC that you have the ability to provide for yourself in Canada.

Funds Required:

The amount of funds required depends on the number of family members. If there is only one person, the amount required is $9,897. See the link below for the requirements if there is more than one person. The exception is if you have arranged employment, you do not have to meet this requirement.

http://www.cic.gc.ca/english/skilled/qual-4.html

Credential Assessment:
If you are highly educated, and had a good career in your homeland, and want help assimilating into the Canadian workforce, it would be helpful, if not necessary, to be assessed for your skill level. One problem that many immigrants face is the fact they have no Canadian work experience. If you go through this assessment process, it could help you to find a job more quickly. The following sites can help you find the information you need:
http://www.cic.gc.ca/english/skilled/work-3.html

Alberta: http://www.advancededucation.gov.ab.ca/iqas/iqas.asp

British Columbia: http://www.bcit.ca/ices/

Manitoba: http://www.gov.mb.ca/labour/immigrate/newcomerservices/7a.html

Ontario: http://www.wes.org/ca/
http://www.wes.org/ca/required/index.asp

Miscellaneous:
http://www.careerbridge.ca/becomeintern.asp
http://www.seecanada.org/see/index.html

6
Business Class

http://www.cic.gc.ca/english/pdf/kits/guides/4000E.PDF
http://www.cic.gc.ca/english/applications/business.html

Investors

http://www.cic.gc.ca/english/business/index.html

- Investors must make a minimum investment in Canada of $400,000 CAD. That investment is used to help participating provinces create jobs and grow their economies. In approximately five years, after you become a permanent resident, your investment is returned to you by the government without interest.

Entrepreneurs

http://www.cic.gc.ca/english/business/index.html

- Entrepreneurs must have business experience, meaning you must have managed or controlled a percent of equity of a qualifying business and your net worth must be at least $300,000 CAD. You must have the intention and ability to start a business within three years in Canada.

Self-Employed

http://www.cic.gc.ca/english/business/index.html

- In this class you must have relevant experience in cultural activities, athletics or farm management. You must also have the intent and ability to start a business, if only to create employment for yourself. No immigration conditions are imposed on this class, but you must have enough money to support yourself and family after you arrive.

7
Provincial Nominee Class

http://www.cic.gc.ca/english/pdf/kits/guides/EP7.pdf
http://www.cic.gc.ca/english/skilled/provnom/index.html

The Provincial Nominee Program allows the provinces and territories to select immigrants who have specific skills that will contribute to the local economy. The Immigration and Refugee Protection Regulations have established the Provincial Nominee Class, allowing provinces that have agreements with CIC to nominate a certain number of foreign nationals for immigration to Canada.

If you have a skill that is needed in a particular province and you want quicker implementation of your immigration application, this class may suit you.

You apply to the province of your choice, as long as it is a participant in the program, and your application is assessed. After you are selected by the province, you then make a formal application to Citizenship and Immigration Canada (CIC), including a letter from the province.

Provincial Nominee applicants are not assessed on the Self-Assessment Test of the Federal Skilled Workers program.

The provinces that currently participate in the program are:
Saskatchewan (1998), British Columbia (1998), Manitoba (1998), New Brunswick (1999), Newfoundland and Labrador (1999), Prince Edward Island (2001), Yukon (2001), Alberta (2002) and Nova Scotia (2002).

Nova Scotia's Provincial Nominee Program (PNP):

The Nova Scotia program has two categories, the Skilled Worker program (the $5,500 fee includes a $1,700 non-refundable application fee) and the Economic program (requires a one-time investment of $128,800). One benefit of this program is that the immigration process is faster, taking approximately six months.

http://www.gov.ns.ca/econ/nsnp/nominee/skilled_worker.asp

8
Family Class

http://www.cic.gc.ca/english/pdf/kits/guides/3900E.pdf
http://www.cic.gc.ca/english/sponsor/index.html

Sponsoring a Family member from Outside of Canada:
http://www.cic.gc.ca/english/sponsor/out.html

Document Checklist:
http://www.cic.gc.ca/english/pdf/kits/forms/IMM5491E.PDF

Sponsoring a Spouse/CLP/Child from Within Canada:
http://www.cic.gc.ca/english/applications/spouse.html
http://www.cic.gc.ca/english/sponsor/in.html
http://www.cic.gc.ca/english/applications/fc.html

Document Checklist:
http://www.cic.gc.ca/english/pdf/kits/forms/IMM5443E.PDF

Note: A new rule was implemented as of February18, 2005 that affects people who are being sponsored by their spouse or partner who are Citizens or permanent residents of Canada.

Sponsoring other family members: (family members may be sponsored after you and your immediate family have already become permanent residents.)

http://www.cic.gc.ca/english/pdf/kits/guides/3998E.PDF
http://www.cic.gc.ca/english/pdf/kits/forms/IMM5287E.PDF

Includes: Parents, grandparents, children adopted outside of Canada or intended to be adopted in Canada, brothers, sisters, nephews, nieces, grandsons or granddaughters who are orphaned, under 18 years of age and not a spouse or common-law partner; or any other family member if there is no spouse, common-law or conjugal partner, son, daughter, mother, father, brother, sister, grandfather, grandmother, aunt, uncle, niece, nephew who is a Canadian citizen or a permanent resident.

Important to Remember when Applying In-Canada:

REMEMBER:	YOU OR YOUR SPOUSE OR COMMON LAW PARTNER:
There is no right of appeal in this category.	Would have to submit an application to a visa office outside Canada to have a right of appeal.
Family Class redesign, which is aimed at faster processing of spouse or common-law partner applications, only applies to applicants outside Canada. Processing times for spouses or common-law partners in Canada are generally longer.	Can apply to a visa office outside Canada to take advantage of the Family Class redesign processing standard or you can find processing times for applications processed in Canada on the CIC website.
Leaving Canada can automatically cancel temporary resident status as a visitor, student or worker.	Have no guarantee that you will be permitted to return or re-enter Canada if you leave before permanent residence is approved. This is especially true if a visitor visa is required.
Applications in this category cannot be transferred to immigration offices outside Canada.	Will have to submit a new application for permanent residence to the Case Processing Centre in Mississauga if you cannot return to Canada[x].

Note: These are the highlights, To see additional requirements for In-Canada applications go to the CIC site listed in the footnote on this page.

9
Same-Sex Partners

Canada is one of the more tolerant countries in the world that has granted various rights to gays and lesbians. Other countries that have recognized same-sex partners include Belgium, Britain, Denmark, Finland, France, Germany, Italy, The Netherlands, Portugal, South Africa, Spain, Sweden, and Switzerland.

The **Canadian Human Rights Act (1996)** - was amended on June 20, section 3(1) to prohibit discrimination on the basis of sexual orientation.

The Modernisation of Benefits and Obligations Act (2000):

http://www.cic.gc.ca/english/press/00/0005%2Dpre.html

This "Act" means that same-sex and common-law partners in Canada will now have the same rights as a married person. This Act has amended 68 federal statutes to extend benefits and obligations to same-sex couples on the same basis as common-law opposite-sex couples (including Old Age Security (OAS), Canada Pension Plan (CPP), and the Income Tax Act (ITA).

Legislative reforms are part of an ongoing commitment by the Government of Canada to ensure that policies and programs continue to reflect the values of Canadians, values that are enshrined in the Canadian Charter of Rights and Freedoms. These rights are about fairness and equal treatment under the law.

Immigration and Refugee Protection Act (the "Act"): (June 28, 2002)

This Act replaced the *Immigration Act 1978*, which was actually conceived in 1976. The 1978 Act was amended more than 30 times and new regulations were added to it to encompass the changes in immigration trends and needs. The new Act was introduced in 2002 as a way of mapping out how Canada wanted the immigration process to look in another decade or so.

The 2002 Act ruling means that same-sex partners and common-law partners can now apply to immigrate to Canada while in the country under the Family Class. Same-sex couples residing abroad can also apply for Permanent Residency together. The couple must meet certain eligibility criteria but they are not required to enter into a formal same-sex marriage.

http://www.cic.gc.ca/english/sponsor/faq-spouse.html
http://www.cic.gc.ca/english/applications/spouse.html
http://www.cic.gc.ca/english/press/05/0504-e.html#backgrounder

21

An Act to Amend the Criminal Code (Hate Propaganda) (2003):

This Bill was passed by the 37th Canadian parliament; it introduces penalties to the Criminal Code of Canada for inciting the hatred of, or encouraging the genocide of, people on the basis of sexual orientation. Prior to this amendment, only action on the basis of race, religion, ethnic origin and colour, gender and disability was protected.

All Canadian provinces and territories prohibit discrimination based on sexual orientation: Alberta (1998 Supreme Court Decision), British Columbia (1992), Manitoba (1987), New Brunswick (1992), Newfoundland/Labrador (1997), Northwest Territories (2002), Nova Scotia (1991), Nunavut (2003), Ontario (1986), Prince Edward Island (1998), Quebec (1997), Saskatchewan (1993), Yukon Territory (1987).

Civil Marriage Act (Bill-C38) (2005):

http://www.parl.gc.ca/common/bills_ls.asp?Parl=38&Ses=1&ls=c38
http://canada.justice.gc.ca/en/fs/ssm/
http://en.wikipedia.org/wiki/Bill_C-38

This Bill was introduced to Parliament on February 1, 2005, and was passed in the House of Commons on June 28, 2005. The Senate gave final approval on July 20, 2005. The Federal enactment of Bill C-38 extends the legal capacity of marriage for civil purposes to same-sex couples in order to reflect values of tolerance, respect and equality to be consistent with the Canadian Charter of Rights and Freedoms.

The Act amends other Acts to ensure that same-sex couples have equal access to the civil rights associated with marriage and divorce. This Bill protects religious institutions by not requiring them to perform same-sex marriages if it is against their religious beliefs.

Through new legislation adopted June 30, 2005 Canada has joined the Netherlands, Belgium, and Spain as the fourth country to legalize same-sex marriage. Canada and Spain offer the least restrictive marriage rights for same-sex couples anywhere in the world. The Netherlands and Belgium, while still leading the way, have some minor limitations involving adoption and children.

http://www.cric.ca/en_html/guide/gay_wedding/gay_wedding.html

Alert to Married Couples Traveling:

http://harolddoan.com/modules.php?name=News&file=article&sid=4690

Provinces with Domestic Partnership Registries (Civil Registry):

http://www.mapleleafweb.com/

Gays and lesbians are now allowed to register as domestic partners in the Provinces of Nova Scotia, Manitoba, and Quebec.

Gays in the Military:

Canada allows gays and lesbians in the military, having lifted the ban in October, 1992 after the Federal court ruled it violated the Canadian Charter of Rights and Freedoms. The first military gay wedding was held in Nova Scotia on May 5, 2005 at Greenwood Air Base.

Timeline of Gay Rights:

http://www.cbc.ca/news/background/samesexrights/timeline_canada.html

An Excellent Resource (LEGIT Vancouver):

http://www.legit.ca/contact.html

10
Citizenship and Immigration Canada

On-Line Services: (CIC)

http://www.cic.gc.ca/english/e-services/index.html

The on-line service allows you to:

- Pay fees by credit card.
- Check the status of your application.
- Change your address.
- Print receipts.

Note: You have the option of requesting a payment form (Form IMM 5401), which must be mailed to you. You then take this form and your payment to a registered Canadian bank to pay the fee. This form cannot be downloaded as it has a unique number and is only available via mail.

To Order Form IMM 5401: (See Order an original receipt)

http://www.cic.gc.ca/english/applications/

Go to the above link and scroll down to "Payment of fees at a financial institution in Canada" (at the bottom of the page). You can also request the forms from this site. You may need several over time so order several.

Fee Schedule:

http://www.cic.gc.ca/english/applications/fees.html#swpf

11
Immigration Fees

When applying in 2002, I paid the following fees:

Total:	(Single applicant)
Application Fee	500.00
Landing Fee	975.00
Visa extensions (2)	150.00
Medical Exam	229.07
2 criminal checks	34.00
3 passport pictures	40.24
Total:	$1,928.31

There are additional fees if you are married, have a family, or if someone is sponsoring you. Be sure to check out the fee schedule at the link below. (Each packet of immigration forms will have a checklist in it that gives you this information.)

Fees: (a few are listed below, see the following website for others)

http://www.cic.gc.ca/english/applications/fees.html#swpf

Family Class:	2005 Fees
Principal Applicant	$475 (non-refundable)
Sponsorship Applicant	$75
Spouse or CLP (over 22)	$550
Family member (under 22)	$150
Business Class:	
Principal Applicant	$1,050
Other Classes:	
Principal Applicant	$550
Work Permit	$150
Temporary Resident Visa	$75 single entry $150 multiple entry
Permanent Residence Fee	$975 (refundable if not accepted)

Note: I sent all my fees in with my application in order to speed things up. All fees must be paid before acceptance is granted. Fees can be paid by cheque, bank draft or money order (personal cheques not accepted).

12
Medical Exam

Every person intending to immigrate to Canada must undergo a medical examination. The Government of Canada publishes a list of approved physicians that you must choose from. Typically you receive a request from CIC to set up your medical after you have applied for immigration.

http://www.cic.gc.ca/english/skilled/before-3.html

I went to a doctor in Halifax (Dalhousie University) and had the following tests: Chest X-ray ($175), blood tests – HIV, Syphilis, Creatinine, urinalysis ($54). I was expected to pay for the chest x-ray at the appointment, but was billed for the blood tests.

The list of approved physicians in the US can be found at:

http://www.cic.gc.ca/english/contacts/dmp/usa.html

The list of approved physicians in Canada can be found at:

http://www.cic.gc.ca/english/contacts/dmp/canada.html

What is meant by "Excessive Demand" and who is exempt?

Excessive Demand refers to a medical or psychological condition that would present a hardship on the Canadian healthcare system. This could deem you medically inadmissible to Canada. The following groups, however, are exempt from inadmissibility on the grounds of excessive demand: individuals who are members of the family class (spouse, common-law partner or a dependent child of the sponsor), convention refugees and protected persons. Such individuals must undertake a medical exam for reasons of public health and public safety only. See OP 15 – Overseas Processing Manual Section 5.7 at following site:

http://www.cic.gc.ca/manuals-guides/english/op/index.html

13
Photos & Criminal Background Check

You will receive instructions to obtain three photos to take to the medical appointment. I had my photos taken at Sears, but any passport photo place can take them (check your yellow pages for Passport Photos). The measurements are specific - between 35 mm x 45 mm (1" by 1 3/8") from chin to crown. The picture size must be 1 3/8" x 1 ¾.

Criminal Background Check and Fingerprinting:

Two full sets of fingerprints (original, not copies, and issued within the last 3 months) are required. In the US, you will be given a PC-1 form to request clearance **from the FBI** and **from your local State police** enforcement agency. A copy of this form is sent, along with the fingerprint cards. You will be asked to give all the addresses you have lived at for more than six months since the age of 18.

A copy of the PC-1 form can be found at:
http://www.cic.gc.ca/english/pdf/kits/guides/E37048.pdf

You can obtain fingerprinting cards from the RCMP office in Canada, or any local police department in the US as long as you show identification.

FBI: One set of original fingerprints is sent to the following address:

> FBI, Criminal Justice Information Services Division (CJIS)
> Attention: SCU Mod D-2
> 1000 Custer Hollow Road
> Clarksburg, WV 26306

The fee is $18, and a certified cheque or money order is required. The cheque is made out to the US Treasury. Explain in a cover letter that you are requesting fingerprints for the purpose of IMMIGRATING TO CANADA. You should receive clearance within three to six weeks, providing you have no past criminal record.

State: One set of original fingerprints is sent to your local officials.

14
Mailing Application & Timeline

If you are applying for Permanent Residence from within the US, your application must be mailed to Buffalo.

If you are applying for travel documents ONLY, from within the US, you can apply to Buffalo, Detroit, Los Angeles, New York, Seattle, Washington, DC.

The address will be in your packet along with your forms. You can also refer to the Document Check List included in your application package for more information.

Where to Send Your Application if Outside of Canada:

Applying from Buffalo:

Canadian Consulate General
Immigration Regional Program Centre
3000 HSBC Center
Buffalo, NY 14203-2884
(716) 858-9500
http://www.cic.gc.ca/english/pdf/kits/guides/E37048.pdf

Where to Send Your Application if applying Outside of Canada and sponsoring your common-law partner or conjugal partner:

Case Processing Centre
P. O. Box 3000 Station A
Mississauga, ON L5A 4N6

Where to Send Your Application if applying Inside of Canada and sponsoring a Spouse or Common-law partner and for Visa extensions:
Case Processing Centre
Vegreville, Alberta T9C 1W3
http://www.cic.gc.ca/english/pdf/kits/guides/5289E.PDF

Application Completion Checklist:

	Read the instructions carefully and follow the directions exactly.
	Complete every blank space on the application, or write N/A (not applicable). Incomplete applications may be returned.
	Follow the checklist included in your application package.
	If you have a job offer in Canada, include the employer's letter.
	If you are not married and trying to prove a relationship include as many supporting documents as possible such as cards, long distance charges, airplane tickets, letters, joint accounts, Will, joint tenancy of a home or property, beneficiary of life insurance, legal documents you both have, emails, pictures, joints bills, lease/rental agreements, and so forth. The more you have the better.
	Add a cover letter and include any information not entered on the application like additional job skills or hobbies or anything you might be able to make a living doing.
	It helps if your job skills are needed in Canada, so take a thorough look at the occupation list to see which job fits your skills. Some give you more points.
	Include job reference letters from former employers.
	Update your resume including ALL jobs and skills you have.
	Include copies of diplomas, transcripts, recognitions & memberships.
	Print out and complete a draft copy. Later, complete the final copy.
	When you are requested to get your medical exam, wait a few weeks and call CIC to make sure they have your results. You may be able to see this on e-client status.
	Make an index of supporting documents. I used post-it flags to separate the sections of my application.
	Organise your application for mailing.
	Recheck the checklist included in your application package and make sure all the necessary documents are included. Include the checklist with your application.
	Finish the application, put it aside and go back to it in a couple days, or have a friend proofread it for accuracy.
	Make a copy of the entire application and send copies, just in case it's lost in the mail. Keep the original for the interview.
	Do not bind the application or the supporting documentation. Use a paper clip to keep the pages together.
	Enclose a money order for the Application and Right of Landing Fees with the application. This saves time later.
	Send the application via FedEx or XpressPost, so you can track it.
	Do not expect much correspondence during the process and do not call CIC unless necessary. I called twice to make sure the application and medical results were received. Expect at least 12 months for processing; it could be much more than this if there is more than one person involved.
	Advise CIC immediately if there are any changes to your application. If you change addresses, you can use the E-client Online Status to notify them.
	Use the E-client Online Status to check your status periodically.
	Make list of personal items to bring into Canada through customs. http://www.cbsa-asfc.gc.ca/E/pbg/cf/b4a/b4a-05b.pdf

My In-Canada Timeline

12/19/01 – Arrived in Canada from Atlanta, Georgia USA.
01/02/02 – Fingerprinted by the local RCMP.
01/08/02 – Sent fingerprints to FBI and GBI (federal and state).
02/08/02 – Medical exam in Halifax ($175) Chest x-ray, blood tests (HIV, Syphilis, Creatinine, and Urinalysis ($54). Took 3 photos ($40).
02/12/02 – Received FBI & GBI clearance.
02/14/02 – Nova Scotia driver's license ($49). Gave up Georgia license.
03/25/02 – Sent Application to Vegreville, Alberta, Xpresspost along with the Receipt IMM 5401 copy 2, showing I had paid fees at the bank in the amount of $1,475 ($975 + $500).
04/12/02 – CIC started processing my application (online status).
05/01/02 – Sent in first extension application $75 (Couples in genuine relationships are now allowed to remain in Canada during the process).
05/06/02 – Confirmed receipt of application & medical results with CIC.
05/22/02 – Received first extension through 12/19/02.
11/01/02 – Received second extension through 12/19/03.
12/03/02 – Received first call from Immigration. They asked 4 questions, then said I would hear from them within 10 days. CIC online status then said "Decision Made".
01/30/03 – Became a Permanent Resident (10 minute apt. in Halifax).
02/07/03 – Mailed application for health card.
02/17/03 – Received Permanent Resident card.
02/18/03 – Received health card.

Average processing time approx. 8-12 months, but could be 36 months.

15
Permanent Resident Status & Citizenship

When you become an official immigrant in Canada you are referred to as a Permanent Resident (formerly a Landed Immigrant) not a citizen.

Rights of a Permanent Resident:

- Live, study and work anywhere in Canada.
- Access to provincial health care card.
- Eligible to apply for citizenship after 3 years.
- Protected by the Canadian Charter of Rights and Freedoms.

Limitations of a Permanent Resident:

- Not allowed to vote.
- Not eligible for certain high-level security jobs.
- May be deported if commit a serious criminal offence.

You can apply to become a citizen of Canada after you have been in Canada for a minimum of three years (1,095 days - the time lived in Canada prior to becoming a Permanent Resident is counted as half).

Information on "How to Become a Citizen" is located at:

http://www.cic.gc.ca/english/citizen/menu-howto.html

Citizenship Fee is $200 (adults): (2005)

http://www.cic.gc.ca/english/applications/fees.html#swpf

16
Dual Citizenship

What the US says:

The US State Department used to be combative in handling dual-citizenship claims. This has changed in recent years, however, and it is much easier to retain this status than it used to be.

The laws forbidding dual citizenship were revoked in 1967 by the US Supreme Court. The court decision was Afroyim v Rusk, as well as a second case in 1980 Vance v Terrazas [xi].

The US Constitution says nothing explicitly about dual citizenship. You will not find an immigration officer in either country who will admit this exists. It is not something that is promoted and you will not be able to call the immigration office to ask how this is done; you will only get a blank stare.

There is no formal application process to apply for Dual Citizenship; it simply happens when you apply for Canadian Citizenship if you do not relinquish your American Citizenship. So, by default, you become a Dual Citizen.

In April 1990, the State Department adopted a new set of much more liberal and streamlined guidelines for handling dual citizenship cases. These guidelines now say it will assume that a US Citizen intends to retain (not give up) his/her US Citizenship if he/she is: naturalized in a foreign country; takes a routine oath of allegiance to a foreign country; or accepts foreign government employment that is of a "non-policy-level" nature.

http://travel.state.gov/law/citizenship/citizenship_778.html

What Canada says:

http://www.voyage.gc.ca/main/pubs/dual_citizenship-en.asp
http://www.cic.gc.ca/english/citizen/dual-info.html
http://www.rsscanadaimmigration.com/en/citizenship/dualcitizenship.php

Canada began allowing dual citizenship on February 15, 1977.

Cross-Border planners recommend that you apply for Canadian Citizenship when you qualify. As a landed immigrant of Canada, this means you must have lived in Canada for a minimum of three years out of the last five to qualify for citizenship.

Canadian/US dual citizens have the best of both worlds and are in no way restricted from living, working or vacationing in either country for any reason throughout their lives [xii].

Your Canadian passport will indicate your dual status.

If you are a person with considerable means, you would be wise to consult with a Cross-Border Tax Planner before becoming a dual citizen.

The real tax advantages of dual citizenship arise when you become a non-resident of Canada and are no longer subject to Canadian tax rules[xiii].

Important When Traveling between Canada/US as a Dual Citizen:

Beginning December 31, 2006, a passport will be required for entering and re-entering the US. This affects visitors to the US and US residents re-entering the US. This first phase affects those traveling by air. The second phase of this requirement goes into affect December 31, 2007 for those traveling by all means of transportation.

In general, a passport is the best identification you can have because it is proof of both citizenship and identity.

Dual citizens should enter the US using US documents only, as you could be fined under US law for entering the US on a foreign passport[xiv]. On your return to Canada you would use your Canadian passport.

International: http://www.newcitizen.us/dual.html
http://www.geocities.com/jusjih/dncdp.html

The US, Israel, UK and Canada currently allow Dual Citizenship[xv].

17
Cross-Border Tax Planning

A US citizen who is a Resident of Canada must file two tax returns annually (one in the US, one in Canada). A foreign tax credit can then be taken to offset taxes paid in another country. This prevents double taxation and is provided for through the US/Canada Tax Treaty (see Chapter 18).

It is important to file your tax returns annually, even if you technically have nothing to report. Some years you may file a return with other forms attached stating that you are taking advantage of this or that treaty.

For example, you are allowed to exclude up to $80,000 USD in foreign wages due to the treaty. You must, however, still file a tax return and report that you are excluding that income.

Tax Forms & Publications: (Main forms you will use)

Canada	United States
T1 General	1040
NS428 (NS) (your Province)	State return (last year only)
Schedule 1 Federal Tax Calculation	1116 Foreign Tax Credit
Schedule 3 Investment Income	8891 RRSP
Schedule 4 Statement of Investment Income	3520
Schedule 5 Dependants	Schedule D
Schedule 9 Donations & Gifts	
Schedule 11 Tuition & Education Amts	**Publications:** **54** Tax Guide for US Citizens Abroad **514** Foreign Tax Credit **593** Tax Highlights for US Citizens & residents abroad

Form TD F 90-22.1:
You are also required to file Form TD F 90-22.1 for amounts in foreign banks totaling over $10,000. This is not associated with your tax form, but is sent separately and due no later than June 30 annually.

http://www.irs.gov/pub/irs-pdf/p4261.pdf
http://www.irs.gov/pub/irs-pdf/f9022-1.pdf

Tax Deadlines:

US – April 15th – You are, however, given an automatic extension until June 15th if you are not in the US on April 15. If you owe tax, it is due by April 15th. An April 15 Canadian postmark does not suffice.

Canada – April 30th - If you are self-employed you have until June 15th; however, if you owe taxes, they must be paid by April 30th.

Filing US Tax Returns:

Filing a tax return is required by law in the US when your world income exceeds the total of your standard deduction ($9,700 in 2004) and personal exemption ($3,100 in 2004). Even if your income does not exceed this amount, it may be advantageous to file anyway. You may be able to reduce your taxes by using the benefits of the treaty. Foreign tax credit planning may help you recover some of the higher taxes paid to Canada on future US returns (unused foreign tax credits can be carried forward for up to five years)[xvi].

Note: Just because you are required to file a US tax return, does not mean you owe tax. There are exemptions and foreign tax credits from taxes paid to Canada for US Citizens living outside of the US that reduce or eliminate tax[xvii].

Other Reasons why it is Important to File US Tax Return:

- To be able to renew your US Passport.
- To collect Social Security benefits when you are eligible.
- May lose rights to tax elections (i.e. to defer income in an RRSP, foreign earned income exclusion, etc.)

35

Cross-Border Planners: (I have experience with the first one only)

http://www.fpanet.org/journal/articles/2001_Issues/jfp1001-art3.cfm

Cross Border Tax and Accounting, LLC
3336 N. 32nd Street, Suite 100
Phoenix, AZ 85018
1 (800) 858-3357
http://www.keatsconnelly.com
(**Note:** Robert Keats is with this firm)

Richard Brunton, CPA
4710 NW Boca Raton Blvd
Boca Raton, FL 33341
1 (561) 241-9991
http://www.taxintl.com

Transition Financial Advisors, Inc.
20 W. Juniper Avenue, Ste 101
Gilbert, AZ 85233
(480) 722-9414
Fax: (480) 812-2090
Email: info@transitionfinancial.com
http://www.transitionfinancial.com

Serbinski Partners, PC
8770 West Bryn Mawr 13flr
Chicago, IL 60631
1 (888) 878-2937
http://www.serbinski.com
http://forums.serbinski.com

KNV Chartered Accountants
#300-15261 Russell Avenue
White Rock, BC V4B2P7
1 (800) 761-7772
http://www.knv.com/Cont.htm

An excellent article entitled **"Taxation of US Citizens Living and/or Working in Canada"** can be found at the Serbinski website below:

http://www.serbinski.com/Amincanada/USTAXChapter.pdf

Information You May Find Helpful in the Future:

Exit Tax - Canada: (established in 1996)

In 1996, Canada established an Exit Tax which means "deemed disposition" occurs (deemed to have sold and repurchased all taxable property you own worldwide even if you did not sell it) when you leave Canada. The Exit tax is not an additional tax, but one you would normally pay when disposing of an appreciated asset. CRA will allow you to defer any tax due upon exit to the date of sale. Proper planning before you leave Canada, however, could help you avoid this altogether[xviii].

Other things you need to do when leaving Canada:

1. Cancel your Canadian Medicare coverage before exiting, or within the grace period, after your departure.
2. Make sure you have US coverage in place. You must be a legal resident of the US before you can exit Canada for tax purposes.
3. Cancel all memberships in Canada.
4. Cancel Canadian credit cards, driver's licenses and vehicle registrations and establish these in the US.
5. Accept no mail deliveries at any address in Canada and have your mail forwarded to the US.
6. Change Wills and other legal documents to reflect US residence.

In other words, you now should act as a visitor in Canada, so that your ties are no longer seen as being in Canada, but in the US where you have moved[xix].

18
US/Canada Tax Treaty

The US and Canada have had a Tax Treaty since the early 1940s, which has been amended and renewed many times since, the most recent being 1997. The purpose of the treaty is to protect people from both countries from incurring double taxation.

The Canada/US Tax Treaty is one of the most important tools used in cross-border financial planning because the terms of the treaty take precedence over almost all the Canadian Income Tax Act rules in Canada and the IRS tax rules in the United States. It is an important trump card to play at appropriate times when doing cross-border planning[xx]. This treaty affects millions of Americans and Canadians.

One of the main things the treaty provides is protection from double taxation. It does this in the following ways:

Foreign Tax Credits – dollar for dollar credit for taxes paid on income in one country when also having to report it in the other country.
Exemptions – For example, exclusion of US$80,000 US of income earned in the other country.

Withholding Rates – the treaty establishes the amount of maximum withholding tax either country can take in various forms of income in that country from residents of the other country[xxi].

The first right of taxation belongs to the country of source and the amount of the tax may be limited by the treaty. The tax credit the other country is obliged to provide is limited to the amount specified by the treaty.

So, Canada must allow a deduction from Canadian tax for income taxes paid or accrued to the US in respect of income that arises in the US, and the US must allow a credit against US tax for income that arises in Canada. (US Form 1116 Foreign Tax Credit; Canada Line 431, 433 on T1 tax form)

To qualify for the exclusion, you must meet the following requirements:

- Your tax home must be outside the US.
- You must be a bona fide resident of a country other than the US.
- Your return must be filed on time.

Some Notable Parts of the Treaty:

Exchange of Information between Countries (Article XXVII):

The Treaty allows tax authorities from both countries to obtain a complete tax profile of anyone who lives in that country. So, it is imperative that you stay in the good graces of the IRS and CCRA by filing tax returns in both countries annually.

"Savings Clause" (Article XXIX):

This "clause" states that the US has the right to tax their residents and citizens; however, there are exceptions listed in paragraph three of this article. I believe that it is only the US that has such a clause in a treaty of this type.

Note: If you hire an accountant, they should be aware that this treaty exists (bear in mind, however, that not all are aware of it). A cross-border planner would be a better choice when seeking advice on taxation issues.

US/Canada Tax Treaty

Articles:	http://www.irs.gov/pub/irs-trty/canada.pdf	(Last negotiated in 1997)
Article I	Personal Scope	
Article II	Taxes Covered	
Article III	General Definitions	
Article IV	Residence	Four rules or tests to determine residency.
Article V	Permanent Establishment	
Article VI	Income from Real Property	
Article VII	Business Profits	No limit. Only taxable in source country if have a permanent establishment in that country.
Article VIII	Transportation	
Article IX	Related Persons	
Article X	Dividends	15% withholding rate unless taxpayer owns at least 10% of the voting stock, in which case the rate is 5%.
Article XI	Interest	10% withholding rate unless the interest is paid by the other country, in which case the interest is exempt from tax in that country (i.e. US Govt Bond interest and Canada Savings Bonds are both exempt in each respective country)
Article XII	Royalties	10% except for certain exempt items in country of source (i.e. copyright royalties or right to use computer software)
Article XIII	Gains	No limit.
Article XIV	Independent Personal Services	No limit, Self-employed income
Article XV	Dependent Personal Services	No limit. However, under $10,000 is exempt, in addition to income

		paid to a person present in the country for 183 days or less by an employer who is a nonresident or has no fixed based in the country.
Article XVI	Artistes and Athletes	
Article XVII	Withholding of Taxes in Respect of Independent Personal Services	
Article XVIII	Pensions and Annuities	15% rate. However, Social Security benefits (including CPP and OAS) are taxable only in the country of residence. Amounts exempt in one country are exempt in the other.
Article XIX	Government Service	Amount paid to its own citizen is taxable only in that country, regardless of where the service is performed.
Article XX	Students	A student training in the other country is exempt from tax on monies received for the education. No limitation on the amount of income or number of years.
Article XXI	Exempt Organizations	
Article XXII	Other Income	
Article XXIII	Capital	
Article XXIV	Elimination of Double Taxation	
Article XXV	Non-Discrimination	
Article XXVI	Mutual Agreement Procedure	
Article XXVII	Exchange of Information	Both countries share tax info
Article XXVIII	Diplomatic Agents and Consular Officers	
Article XXIX	Miscellaneous Rules	Savings Clause
Article XXX	Entry Into Force	
Article XXI	Termination	

41

Other Countries' Treaties with Canada:

http://www.fin.gc.ca/treaties/treatystatus_e.html

19
Foreign Tax Credit - Double Taxation

Tax planning that involves two countries is complex. It may be useful to hire a cross-border planner who specialises in this area of tax, and who understands the US/Canada Tax Treaty.

US: Form 1116 Foreign Tax Credit

http://www.irs.gov/pub/irs-pdf/i1116.pdf

There are three main categories of income: Passive, General Limitation and High Tax Withholding. You must claim the credit in the year the income is generated. The credit may then be carried back two years or forward five years. After this time, the credit expires. You must also report each type of income on a separate Form 1116.

The formula for calculating foreign tax credit is difficult and limits you to so much per year. It is based on a ratio of your total income outside the US as compared to your worldwide income including the US.

$$\frac{\text{Net Foreign Income}}{\text{Net Income}} \times \text{Federal Tax payable} = \text{Federal Tax Payable}$$

Example: Matt's taxable income is $25,000. It is made up of $20,000 Canadian income, plus $5,000 interest from a foreign country. The foreign country withheld $500 in tax, which is the full extent of Matt's foreign tax liability. Matt's federal tax (before taking any foreign tax credit into account) is $2,600. His federal foreign tax credit is therefore the lesser of:
$500, the foreign tax paid; and
$520, calculated as $5,000/$25,000 x $2,600.

So, Matt can deduct $500 from his basic federal tax, reducing it from $2,600 to $2,100. As a result, his total tax liability (both Canadian and foreign) is no greater than if he had earned the money in Canada. In this example Matt was able to deduct all of the foreign tax paid from his federal tax. This, however, is not always the case.

43

Publication 514:   http://www.irs.gov/publications/

You can download this IRS publication at the above site. It will give you details on the Foreign Tax Credit for Individuals and more examples.

Example of a Retired US Citizen living in Canada:

Go to: http://www.centa.com/articles/U.S.Cdntaxation.htm
Scroll down to near the bottom where it says "EXAMPLE" and read the scenario of how this person's taxes were calculated.

Other Resources:

http://www.cra-arc.gc.ca/E/pub/tp/it270r3/README.html

http://fiducial.soho.cch.com/complete-tax/text/c60s10d453.asp

http://www.cra-arc.gc.ca/E/pbg/tf/t2209/README.html

20
Tax Differences – US and Canada

	CANADA	US
Personal Exemptions	Converts the basic personal exemption to a non-refundable federal tax credit at the current lowest tax bracket rate of 16% (2004).	Standard Deduction or Itemized Deduction can be claimed.
Pensions	$1,000 pension deduction converted to a non-refundable federal tax credit at the current lowest tax rate 16% (2004).	No standard pension deduction. Social Security payments are completely tax-free until income exceeds a certain amount, then taxed at 50%, then 85% (Top tax rate is 30%).
Mortgage Interest & Property Tax	Not deductible. Gains on sale of a Principal Residence are tax-free.	Mortgage Interest on as many as two homes is fully deductible as an itemized deduction on Form 1040 Schedule A&B.
Provincial/State Income Tax	Provincial taxes can't be deducted from federal taxes paid.	State and Municipal taxes are deductible as an itemized deduction on Form 1040 Schedule A&B.
Capital Gains Deduction	Qualifying Small Business Owners have a $500,000 capital gains exemption on the sale of shares of a company. Capital gains inclusion rate is currently 50%.	Capital Gains are taxed at reduced rates with a maximum of 15%. A Capital Gains exemption of $250,000 applies to the sale of a principal residence if owned for minimum of 2 years.
Medical Expenses **(2004)**	Over 3% of income is converted to a non-refundable credit	Expenses that exceed 7.5% of your adjusted gross income are deductible as an

	at the lowest tax rate of 16%	itemized deduction.
Registered Retirement Plans	Canadians with earned income can contribute 18% of last year's earnings to an RRSP each year, up to a maximum which is $15,500 (2005).	Americans with earned income can contribute up to the lesser of 100% of their income or $4,000 to their own, and $4,000 to a spouse's IRA (2005). A Roth IRA is subject to the same limits above, but is not deductible from taxable income because these contributions are made pre-tax. Earnings are tax-free inside the plan and at withdrawal.
Charitable Donations (2004)	Donations can't exceed 75% of income to Qualified Canadian charities. Allowed as a non-refundable tax credit at 16% of the first $250 and 29% of the remainder.	Donations cannot exceed 50% of income and is allowed as an itemized deduction.
Education Plan	Canadians can contribute up to $4,000 per child under age 18 to an RESP each year. Income is tax deferred until withdrawn, and then is taxed to the student. The Canada Education Savings Grant (CESG) can add 20% per year	Americans can contribute to an Educational IRA of up to $3,000 per child per year that accumulates on a tax-deferred basis. There are several refundable tax credits to encourage low-income persons to attend college. States have 529 College Savings Plans whereby parents and

	to an RESP with an annual limit of $400 and a lifetime limit of $7,200.	grandparents can contribute up to $275,000. Earned income is tax-free if used for college expenses. These plans are more flexible than the Canadian RESP.
Miscellaneous Deductions	Union and Professional Dues, safety deposit box fees (if used to store investments), interest on funds borrowed for investment purposes and fees for investment advice are deductible. (Note: fees paid to a Financial Planner to prepare a financial plan are not deductible.)	Tax prep fees, vehicle licenses, property and casualty losses exceeding 10% of income, unreimbursed employment expenses, trustee fees, safety deposit box fees, interest on funds borrowed for investment purposes, IRA administration fees, and fees for financial planning/investment advice (2% rule applies).

21
Social Security Benefits

http://www.ssa.gov/pubs/10137.html
http://www.ssa.gov/foreign/canada.htm
http://www.ssa.gov/OP_Home/handbook/ssa-hbk.htm
http://www.ssa.gov/international/Agreement_Pamphlets/canada.html

A US Citizen living in Canada will receive US social security payments. Following are the details:

Requirements:	Forty quarters of coverage qualifies you to receive Medicare. Part A (Hospital) benefits free at age 65. You would then pay $200 annually (approximately) for Part B (Medical Insurance) coverage. It is recommended that you pay for Part B coverage because if you travel it is cheaper than buying travel insurance.
Suggested:	Request a Social Security Statement of Benefits before you leave the US http://www.ssa.gov/mystatement
How Reported on Tax Returns:	You report the full amount on Line 115 of your Canadian return (T1). Deduct 15% on Line 256. So you are only taxed on 85% of the benefit and only in Canada. You do not report any of this on the US 1040 Return. **Rule:** Report this income only in the Country of residence. (US/Canada Tax Treaty – Article XVIII, Paragraph 5). **Note:** The taxable portion qualifies for the Pension Income Non-Refundable Credit on your Canadian T1 (Schedule 1 Line 330).
OAS Benefits	At age 65, all residents of Canada qualify for the OAS (Old Age Security). This benefit is also only taxable in your country of residence and should not be included on the US 1040 Return.
CPP Benefits	At age 60, a person who has worked in Canada and contributed to the CPP (Canada Pension Plan) along with other requirements of time can get a CPP pension. This, too, is only taxed in the country of residence and should not be included on the US 1040 Return.

22
Medical Coverage in the US

A US Citizen who moves to Canada has access to both Canadian and US medical coverage and doctors if you are over 65 (or 62 if you collect SS early) and have qualified for US Medicare. You retain medical coverage even as a resident of Canada.

You will have access to the Canadian medical system through your Provincial Medicare and to the US Medical system through US Medicare. If you live near the border (and even if you do not) and you need surgery and cannot get it quickly enough in Canada due to long waiting lists, you can go to the US, have the surgery and be fully covered.

Another advantage is if you want to vacation or travel to the US, your US Medicare gives you very economical travel insurance; there is no restriction by age or medical condition.

Medicare is two part: A & B. "Part A" covers hospital care and **"Part B" covers doctors and outpatient care.** If you have obtained the minimum forty quarters, then your Part A is free. You will pay a minimal amount for Part B coverage, approximately $70 per month. If you plan to travel back to the US periodically, it would be cheaper to pay this premium than to purchase travel insurance (see Chapter 21).

The US Medicare system has no rules requiring you to be present in the US for a certain time period each year, so you do have the best of both worlds[xxii].

For general information on the costs and types of healthcare plans in the US, refer to the website of the US Agency for Healthcare Research and Quality and the others below:

http://www.ahrq.gov/consumer/

http://www.ehealthinsurance.com/ehi/index.html

http://www.healthchoices.org/

23
Healthcare in Canada

Health care in Canada is a Universal Healthcare system whereby all residents have access to services. Healthcare matters come under provincial jurisdiction and are based on the minimum requirements of the federal Canada Health Act[xxiii].

The Canadian government shares approximately one-half of the cost of the provincial plans (Quebec is the exception). Each Province decides, within certain parameters, what services are provided and whether or not a premium is paid by residents. Some Provinces refer to this as **MSI (Medical Services Insurance)**; others call it **MSP (Medical Services Plan).** A premium is charged in three Provinces for basic services.

Basic Medical Services:
- Examination and treatment by family doctors.
- Many types of surgery.
- Most treatment by specialists, upon referral.
- Anaesthesia services.
- X-rays and other diagnostic procedures.
- Many laboratory tests.
- Most immunizations.
- Maternity services.

Basic Hospital Services:

- Accommodation in public ward levels and meals.
- Necessary in-hospital nursing services.
- Laboratory, x-ray, other diagnostic procedures.
- Medications administered.
- Operating room use and anaesthesia.
- Routine surgical supplies.
- Use of radiotherapy facility.
- Services rendered by employees of the hospital.

Health-care services not covered by Medicare, and for which you have to pay include: (the alternative is to purchase an Extended Health Plan):

- Medical exams for employment, visas, passport, etc.
- Ambulance services.
- Prescription drugs.
- Dental care.
- Glasses and contact lenses.

- Cosmetic surgery.
- Advice by telephone.
- Hospital charges for private or semi-private accommodations.

Extended Health Benefit Plans can be purchased to cover expenses in excess and those not covered by basic benefits from the following companies: **Blue Cross, Green Shield, Manulife, Sun Life, Great West (Sonata)**. http://www.insurance-canada.ca/index.php.

If you have a pre-existing condition, many of these companies will not cover your current drugs in use, or will charge you an extra premium after underwriting. These services are sometimes covered by workplace benefit packages.

Your health insurance card is mainly for use in the province where you live. If you are visiting another province and have a medical emergency, you can use your card. If you move to another province, however, you will need to apply for a new card. As mentioned previously, one of the first things that should be done once you are accepted as a permanent resident of Canada, is to apply for your medical insurance card.

Note: In certain provinces, the services of other medical practitioners are covered as well, but benefits are limited (chiropractor, podiatrist, physiotherapist, naturopath, optometrist, orthopedist, osteopath). If you are covered, however, you are restricted to a certain dollar maximum per visit and a maximum per year. In Nova Scotia, for example, an optometrist is covered, but only for persons under age 18 or over age 65. Those receiving income security are also included. Check with your province for further information.

51

Provincial Healthcare – Basic Plan Benefits: (applications can be found on the websites)

Provinces:	Healthcare Websites:	Waiting Period	Premium
Alberta (AHCIP)	http://www.health.gov.ab.ca/ahci p/forms.html http://www.university.ca/eng/can adainfo/healthcare/albhealth.htm #premandrate	0	Yes (over $7,560 taxable income – if Single)
British Columbia (MSP)	http://www.healthservices.gov.bc .ca/msp/index.html http://www.healthservices.gov.bc .ca/msp/infoben/premium.html	3 months	Yes
Manitoba (MH)	http://www.gov.mb.ca/health/mh sip/index.html	0	
New Brunswick	http://www.gnb.ca/0051/index-e.asp	3 months	
Newfoundland	http://www.health.gov.nl.ca/healt h	0	
Nova Scotia (MSI)	http://www.gov.ns.ca/heal/msi.ht m	0	
Ontario (OHIP)	http://www.health.gov.on.ca/engl ish/public/program/ohip/ohip_m n.html	3 months	Yes (over $20,000 taxable income)
Quebec	http://www.ramq.gouv.qc.ca/en/c itoyens/carte/index.shtml	3 months	
Territories:			
Yukon	http://www.hss.gov.yk.ca	0	
NW Territory	http://www.hlthss.gov.nt.ca	0	
Nunavut	http://www.gov.nu.ca/hss.htm	0	

Waiting Lists for Procedures:

http://www.fraserinstitute.ca/shared/readmore.asp?sNav=pb&id=705

For example: My friend needs a knee replacement and her waiting time for surgery is two years. This is the reality for some non-emergency medical procedures.

Health Insurance –While Awaiting Immigration Decision:

No healthcare coverage is available in Canada until you are officially a permanent resident. Once you become a permanent resident you will still have a three month waiting period in some provinces. You will, therefore, need to purchase interim coverage for you and your family.

Resources:

http://www.insurancetogo.com/

http://www.canadasure.com/about.php3

http://www.expatriate-insurance.com/

http://www.imglobal.com/ (I purchased interim insurance here)

http://www.trenthealth.com/include/Consumers.asp

http://www.canadian-family-medical-plans.com/medical_canadian_visitors.htm

Note: You need to purchase travel insurance when you visit the US, as your provincial coverage is minimal when out of the country. (Bear in mind that if you are out of most provinces for more than 6 months, you are at risk of losing your medical plan: Ontario – 7 months, Newfoundland – 8 months)

24
Healthcare – Comparing the US and Canada

USA	CANADA
* Private hospitals compete for patients.	* Publicly funded hospitals; however, some private clinics are starting to pop-up offering MRIs due to the long waiting lists. Those who can afford to pay get them earlier. The Supreme Court of Canada has seen some cases lately.
* Too much money is spent on administering complicated health plans and the multiple insurers each make up their own rules as to coverage.	* Since administration is so simple, the majority of the funding goes directly to providing healthcare services to its citizens and permanent residents.
* Health costs account for 14% of GDP, yet 45 million Americans have no health insurance or very limited coverage.	* Health costs account for 10% of GDP and this provides full coverage for all citizens.
* Insurers play games and stall to avoid paying bills and constantly question bills, sending them back to the doctors for explanation.	* The billing system is as simple as sending an invoice to the Ministry of Health in Ottawa, which pays on a fee-for-service basis.
* The poor without coverage do not seek care until their problems have become serious.	* Canadians are healthier with a longer lifespan and lower infant mortality rates.
* More hospital beds per person are available.	* Hospitals do not fund excess capacity.
* The US system is experiencing soaring costs and is in a state of disrepair.	* The Canadian system is also in need of reform due to the aging population and is experiencing shortfalls in cash and medical staff due to doctors (primarily specialists and surgeons) approaching retirement. This is a current priority of the Canadian government.
* Co-pays and deductibles are common in the US, along with many having to pay out of pocket for their medical premiums if they are not covered by their employers.	* The Provinces were unified over 20 years ago and all adhere to basic principles including: nationwide acceptance of each plan, comprehensive coverage, no out-of-pocket costs (co-pays/deductibles) for insured services to name a few.

* Soaring drug costs and an aging population.	* Soaring drug costs and an aging population. Drugs, however, are cheaper in Canada as witnessed by the many online drugstores selling to Americans.
* The wealthy can go anywhere to get the medical services they need because they have the funds to pay.	* One cannot bribe a doctor to do surgery after hours (for example) due to the equal-access-for-all principle which says paying for insured services is illegal.
* The US is the only developing nation without universal healthcare.	* Canadians spend much less on medical care.
	* The system periodically loses physicians to the USA who are lured by higher pay and lower taxes. Many return to Canada, however, due to the excessive paperwork and bureaucracy in the States, as well as the need to collect bills from patients.

25
Things to do on Arrival in Canada

Priority:
- Apply for Medical Services Card – (See Chapter 23).
- Apply for SIN (Social Insurance Number) - (See Chapter 26).

Other:
- Obtain a Driver's License - You will have to turn in your US license (I asked for a copy to keep). In Nova Scotia, a visitor is allowed to drive for 90 days if you are in possession of a valid license from your home province or country. Check with the Registry of Motor Vehicles in your province, as each province makes their own rules and some require a driver's test. I was not required to take a test. The fee was $45. The fee is now $63.60 for Class 5 regular driver's license. The license is good for 5 years (See Nova Scotia site below). http://www.gov.ns.ca/snsmr/rmv/registration/register.asp
- **Housing** (see Chapter 27)
- **Education** (see Chapter 31)
- **Utility Hookups** - http://www.utilityconnection.com/page3x.html

You Might have a Canadian Attorney draw up the following Legal Documents:

- Estate Plan.
- Will.
- Living Will.
- Enduring Powers of Attorney (POAs) for general matters and medical.

Other Suggestions:

- Keep a small checking/savings account in the US to cover incidentals.
- Keep one credit card to use for incidentals or when you travel there or just to keep your credit rating active.

26
Social Insurance Card (SIN)

The SIN card is similar to the Social Security card in the US. It is recommended that you apply for this card as soon as you receive permanent resident status. Since you have to show them your status documents, it is best that you take the completed application with your official documents to a local Human Resources Social Development Canada (HRSDC) office and apply in person. This will prevent having to send important documents through the mail. You should receive your card within approximately 3 weeks.

An application can be downloaded at the following site:

http://www.sdc.gc.ca/en/gateways/nav/top_nav/our_offices.shtml#01

Credentials needed to apply for a SIN card:

You must provide a primary document that proves your status in Canada, as well as a supporting document if the name on your primary document is different from the one you are currently using. The documents must be originals written in English or French.

Primary Documents:

- Record of Landing (ROL).
- Confirmation of Permanent Residence.
- Supporting document: (if necessary).
- Marriage certificate or marriage registration.
- Divorce Decree.
- Legal change of name document.
- Adoption papers certified by a Canadian Court.
- Request to Amend Immigration Record of Landing or confirmation of permanent residence.

57

Human Resources Social Development Canada (HRSDC) offices for each province: (Similar to Social Services in the US)

Provinces:	Websites:
Alberta	http://www.sdc.gc.ca/en/gateways/where_you_live/regions/offices/ab-nwt-nu.shtml
British Columbia	http://www.sdc.gc.ca/en/gateways/where_you_live/regions/offices/bc-yk.shtml
Manitoba	http://www.sdc.gc.ca/en/gateways/where_you_live/regions/offices/mb.shtml
New Brunswick	http://www.sdc.gc.ca/en/gateways/where_you_live/regions/offices/nb.shtml
Newfoundland	http://www.sdc.gc.ca/en/gateways/where_you_live/regions/offices/nl.shtml
Nova Scotia	http://www.sdc.gc.ca/en/gateways/where_you_live/regions/offices/ns.shtml
Ontario	http://www.sdc.gc.ca/en/gateways/where_you_live/regions/offices/on.shtml
PEI	http://www.sdc.gc.ca/en/gateways/where_you_live/regions/offices/pe.shtml
Quebec	http://www.sdc.gc.ca/en/gateways/where_you_live/regions/offices/qc.shtml
Saskatchewan	http://www.sdc.gc.ca/en/gateways/where_you_live/regions/offices/sk.shtml
Territories:	
Yukon	http://www.sdc.gc.ca/en/gateways/where_you_live/regions/offices/bc-yk.shtml
NW Territory	http://www.sdc.gc.ca/en/gateways/where_you_live/regions/offices/ab-nwt-nu.shtml
Nunavut	http://www.sdc.gc.ca/en/gateways/where_you_live/regions/offices/ab-nwt-nu.shtml

27
Housing

In Canada, when you sell your home, as long as it is your Principal Residence, any gains are non-taxable. This, however, does not apply to cottages or other homes referred to as Personal Use properties.

http://www.grantthornton.ca/mgt_papers/MIP_template.asp?MIPID=116
http://www.cra-arc.gc.ca/E/pub/tp/it120r6/it120r6-01-e.html

2005 Reports on Housing and Pricing in Canada:

http://www.remax-oa.com/roafiles/marketreports/forecast2005_pr.pdf
http://www.royallepage.ca/CMSTemplates/GlobalNavTemplate.aspx?id=361

Housing - Multiple Listings: http://www.mls.ca

The housing market in Canada has been good the last few years, as there has been a flurry of building of new homes. Since the interest rates have been low for a long time, this has given individuals incentive to invest in a home. The rates are not expected to rise in the coming year.

Most expensive housing market in Canada – Vancouver, Toronto, Victoria, Montreal and Ottawa.

Least Expensive Cities in Canada:

Moncton, Saskatchewan, Charlottetown, Winnipeg, St. John's.

Nova Scotia – Inexpensive Place to Live:

http://www.nsliving.info/

Newcomers Guide:
http://www.cic.gc.ca/english/newcomer/guide/index.html

CMHC Newcomers Guide to Housing: (Canada Mortgage & Housing Corp)
https://www.cmhc-schl.gc.ca

Renting a Home Guide:

http://www.cmhc-schl.gc.ca/en/bureho/reho/yogureho/index.cfm

Apartment Listings by Province:

http://www.apartmentscanada.com/

Monthly Living Expenses: (for family of 3)

http://www.settlement.org/sys/faq_print.asp?passed_lang=EN&faq_id=4000204

28
Weather in Canada

http://www.weatheroffice.ec.gc.ca/canada_e.html

Yes, the winters are cold in Canada but there are four seasons.

The temperature is measured in Celsius rather than Fahrenheit. To convert from Celsius to Fahrenheit, double the Celsius number and add 30. If the Celsius number is a minus number (Celsius x 1.8) + 32 = Fahrenheit. For example:

8 Celsius = approximately 46 Fahrenheit

-2 Celsius = approximately 35 Fahrenheit

Average Temperatures in Canada:

http://members.tripod.com/~MitchellBrown/almanac/temp_morning.html

Weather Almanac in Canada:

http://members.tripod.com/~MitchellBrown/almanac/index.html

29
Canadian Residency Requirements

Understanding what makes you a Resident of Canada:

- Spending more than 183 days in any year in Canada.
- Regular and lengthy visits to Canada.
- Having personal property in Canada.
- Social ties.
- A telephone listing.
- Driver's license.
- Health coverage.
- Home.
- Bank accounts and investments.

Canada taxes its "residents" based on world income earned. Canada has no income tax laws dealing with the taxation of non-residents. If you are no longer a resident of Canada, you are not taxed on world income. There is, however, an Exit Tax you will pay when you leave the country (see Chapter 17).

Maintaining Permanent Residency:

Canada has the most flexible residency requirements in the world. A permanent resident must be in Canada only for an accumulated 730 days (not required to be consecutive) out of any five year period. So you can be outside of Canada for up to three years in any given 5 year period and not lose your status.

Time spent working for a Canadian company outside Canada (or accompanying a spouse who is working in the same situation) also counts towards keeping your permanent residence.

30
Credit Rating & Banking Issues

Equifax Canada
Box 190 Jean Talon Station
Montreal, Quebec
H1S 2Z2
1 800 465-7166
http://www.equifax.ca

Equifax US
P. O. Box 740241
Atlanta, GA 30374-0241
1 (800) 685-1111
http://www.equifax.com

Note: Trans Union Credit http://www.transunion.com and Experian http://www.experian.com are credit reporting agencies; both are in Canada.

Credit Report:

It would be a good idea to request a credit report before you leave the US as you want to make sure it is correct. Then you can bring a copy of it with you. You can order one at this website: http://www.equifax.com/

You might even ask your current banker to give you a letter of credit experience with that bank before you leave the US.

Credit Rating:

Since moving to a new country automatically means you will have no credit rating in that country, the following tips may help in how to approach this issue when approaching a Canadian bank to open an account or to get a mortgage.

Give the bank your US social security number and ask them to contact Equifax in the US to inquire about your credit history. Or, you could show them a copy of the credit report you received before leaving the US.

Credit Cards:

- American Express is currently the only credit card company that will transfer your account to Canada.
- If you open an account at a bank in Canada, most of the time you can get a credit card if you have your permanent resident papers, licenses, and so forth for identification.
- 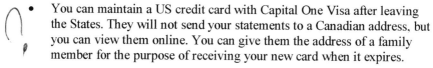 You can maintain a US credit card with Capital One Visa after leaving the States. They will not send your statements to a Canadian address, but you can view them online. You can give them the address of a family member for the purpose of receiving your new card when it expires.

Mortgage:

http://www.cba.ca/en/viewPub.asp?fl=6&sl=23&docid=29&pg=1

- Ask local people who they would recommend.
- Consult a Mortgage Broker who knows the US and Canadian markets.
- TD Bank has been known to give a mortgage/line of credit based on your salary in Canada. Show them your employment contract and permanent resident application form for proof that you have a job in Canada and are a legal resident.

Bank Account:

- TD Bank seems to have the best understanding of the situation that new immigrants to Canada are faced with.
- I chose to open an account with Royal Bank. I then opened a US account with their affiliate, RBC Centura which is located in North Carolina. You can do all of your banking online through the website of both banks. The RBC Centura Royal Embassy checking account has a minimum balance $700 (or pay $3.95 mthly), Online Bill Pay/Web Banking, free ATM Card which you can use at any Cirrus, Interlink, Star ATM in Canada or US. They give you one free monthly cross-border transfer from the Royal Bank to your Centura account in the US. There is no US cash exchange fee when traveling in the US and you are entitled to a reduced foreign bank ATM fee up to two ($2 US) credits per withdrawal when using Cirrus, Interlink or Star ATMs.

- There is no problem with having a bank account in both countries, as it does not signify residency. I keep a small bank account and a credit card in the US for incidentals and to help out my mother from time to time. I have found numerous occasions where I was glad I did, so I highly recommend others to do it too.

Note: When opening the new account in Canada, it is best to bring documentation with you, for example your passport, landing papers, driver's license, a bank statement from the US, latest pay slip and maybe an employer verification letter from your former employer in the US.

Ways to help establish credit in new country:

- Money in a new bank account.
- Apply for and use a credit card, but pay it off regularly.
- Apply for a small car loan (for example) and pay it off on time.
- Subscribe to a magazine.
- Order items online and always pay them off immediately.

31
Education in Canada

Contact information for all the Provincial and Territorial Departments and Ministries responsible for education in Canada can be found at the following website:

http://www.cmec.ca/educmin.en.stm
http://www.canadianembassy.org/education/studyincanada-en.asp

The Education System in Canada:

http://www.studycanada.ca/english/education_system_canada.htm

http://www.cicic.ca/postsec/volume2/indexe.stm

http://www.educationcanada.cmec.ca/EN/home.php

Terminology Used in Education & Universities in Canada:

http://www.uwaterloo.ca/canu/

Comparative Study of Education in the US and other G8 Countries: (ED484514)

http://www.eric.ed.gov/ERICWebPortal/Home.portal

Go to the above website and **do a search on ED484514**. This will go to the study title above. This study was conducted in 2004 and is comprehensive in comparing the education system in many countries with that of Canada.

32

Importing Personal Items to Canada

Custom Tips – Entering Canada by Car:
http://gocanada.about.com/library/howto/htcustomsbycar.htm

Personal Items: http://www.cbsa-asfc.gc.ca/E/pub/cp/rc4151/README.html

- It might be easier to sell certain personal items before you leave your country of origin and buy them again once you arrive in Canada. This will make moving across the border much easier. For example, I sold my car and furniture and gave some clothing to Goodwill.
- These are duty exempt for Permanent Residents landing (make up a list).
- Do not go out and buy any new items to bring to Canada with you – I believe you must have owned the items for at least one year to be exempt from duty.

Importing a Vehicle into Canada:

http://www.cbsa.gc.ca/E/pub/cp/rc4140/rc4140-02e.pdf
http://www.riv.ca/english/html/how_to_import.html

Car Modifications that May be Required:

http://www.riv.ca/english/html/mod_inspect_requirements.html

List of Cars Allowed and Not Allowed:

http://www.riv.ca/english/US_vehicle_admissibility.pdf

Licensing:

http://www.riv.ca/english/html/provincial_licensing.html

Car Insurance: http://www.kanetix.com

33
Employment in Canada

http://www.hrsdc.gc.ca/en/gateways/topics/hxe-gxr.shtml
http://www.canadaimmigrationvisa.com/oejs.html#hrdc
http://www.statcan.ca/english/freepub/89-611-XIE/labour.htm

HRSDC (Human Resources Social Development Canada):

HRSDC is the labour department of Canada. One of its main functions is to ensure that Canadian companies hire foreign workers only if the job vacancy cannot be filled by a Canadian permanent resident or citizen either due to a shortage of manpower or lack of qualifications or skills to do the job. If a company hires a foreign worker and is supporting their permanent immigration, in most cases HRSDC must issue a LMO (Labour Market Opinion)[xxiv]. There are exemptions from the LMO for certain job skills[xxv].

Canada's unemployment rate is around 7%, which is low on the international scale. It may be initially difficult, however, to get a job unless your particular skills are needed and there is no Canadian citizen available to fill the position. If at all possible, try to find a job before you come to Canada, as this will make your transition much easier. The alternative is to have plenty of money to support you and your family until you find a job.

Many professionals say their credentials from their homeland are not good enough and that they must go through further training in Canada to do the same job they may have been doing for years; be aware of this! (See Chapter 5)

The good news is that Canada knows this is a problem and some provinces like Nova Scotia are now establishing a method to assess the credentials of physicians who are trained in other countries, so that those people can fill shortages in the province. Hopefully, more provinces will follow and create assessment programs for other types of jobs.

If you move to a rural area, some good jobs can be hard to find. Even if you do find a job, the wages are low; typically the minimum wage of $6.50 per hour.

The immigration process gives higher points for higher education, but then doesn't provide much help in finding those types of jobs once you arrive. Many in rural areas are self-employed, so if you have skills you can earn a living doing, then this is probably your best option in the rural areas. Give this some thought.

Important Factors Employers look for:

- Language skills.
- Current and diversified professional skills.
- Interpersonal/multitasking abilities.
- Motivation/work ethic/initiative are highly valued.
- Know-how to sell and promote your knowledge, skills & personal traits.
- A good work ethic.

Challenges:

* Canadian employers require Canadian work experience (to get around this you may ask to volunteer initially to show a company your skills and qualifications).

* Many immigrants go to the larger cities like Toronto, Montreal and Vancouver, so these markets are typically flooded with immigrants. You might try going to a smaller province and town in Alberta, Manitoba, New Brunswick or Nova Scotia initially. Just be sure your skills are needed there and that you have a job lined up

NAFTA: http://www.cic.gc.ca/english/pub/you-asked/section-18.html

http://www.hrsdc.gc.ca/asp/gateway.asp?hr=/en/on/epb/fwp/faq_sales_service.shtml&hs=hxe

NAFTA and Nursing Jobs:

http://www.hrsdc.gc.ca/asp/gateway.asp?hr=/en/on/epb/fwp/nurse_nafta.shtml&hs
=hxe

Temporary Foreign Worker Guidelines:

http://www.cic.gc.ca/manuals-guides/english/fw/index.html

Academics:

http://www.hrsdc.gc.ca/asp/gateway.asp?hr=/en/on/epb/fwp/fwp_hand00.shtml&h
s=hxe

Where to Get Training:

http://www.labourmarketinformation.ca/standard.asp?ppid=86&lcode=E&prov=&
gaid=&occ=&search_key=1&pre_sel_criteria=0

HRSDC – Employment by Province: http://www.hrsdc.gc.ca/en/home.shtml

PROVINCES:	WEBSITES:
Alberta	http://www.hrsdc.gc.ca/en/gateways/where_you_live/regions/ab-nwt-nu.shtml
British Columbia	http://www.hrsdc.gc.ca/en/gateways/where_you_live/regions/bc-yk.shtml
Manitoba	http://www.hrsdc.gc.ca/en/gateways/where_you_live/regions/mb.shtml
New Brunswick	http://www.hrsdc.gc.ca/en/gateways/where_you_live/regions/nb.shtml
Newfoundland & Labrador	http://www.hrsdc.gc.ca/en/gateways/where_you_live/regions/nl.shtml
Nova Scotia	http://www.hrsdc.gc.ca/en/gateways/where_you_live/regions/ns.shtml
Ontario	http://www.hrsdc.gc.ca/en/gateways/where_you_live/regions/on.shtml
PEI	http://www.hrsdc.gc.ca/en/gateways/where_you_live/regions/pe.shtml
Quebec	http://www.hrsdc.gc.ca/en/gateways/where_you_live/regions/qc.shtml
Saskatchewan	http://www.hrsdc.gc.ca/en/gateways/where_you_live/regions/sk.shtml
Territories:	
Yukon	http://www.hrsdc.gc.ca/en/gateways/where_you_live/regions/bc-yk.shtml
NW Territory	http://www.hrsdc.gc.ca/en/gateways/where_you_live/regions/ab-nwt-nu.shtml
Nunavut	http://www.hrsdc.gc.ca/en/gateways/where_you_live/regions/ab-nwt-nu.shtml

Employment Prospects by Province:

http://www.labourmarketinformation.ca/standard.asp?ppid=57&lcode=E&prov=&gaid=&occ=&search_key=1&pre_sel_criteria=0

Employers Who Hire: (use this interactive database to find a job)

http://www.labourmarketinformation.ca/standard.asp?ppid=59&lcode=E&prov=&
gaid=&occ=&search_key=1&pre_sel_criteria=0

Compare Occupations:

http://www.labourmarketinformation.ca/standard.asp?ppid=94&lcode=E&prov=&
gaid=&occ=&search_key=1&pre_sel_criteria=0

Hiring Temporary Foreign Workers in Canada: (Hiring Steps)

http://www.hrsdc.gc.ca/asp/gateway.asp?hr=en/epb/lmd/fw/tempoffers.shtml&hs=
hxe

International Salary Calculator: (find out the equivalent of your salary in Canada)

http://www.homefair.com/homefair/servlet/ActionServlet?pid=500&homefair&to
=ActionServlet%3Fpid%3D244%26cid%3Dhomefair&pagename=199&internal=
T

Wages and Salaries:

http://www.labourmarketinformation.ca/standard.asp?ppid=43&lcode=E&prov=&
gaid=&occ=&search_key=1&pre_sel_criteria=0

Minimum Wage: (by Province as of 09/01/2005)

http://canadaonline.about.com/gi/dynamic/offsite.htm?site=http://www.gov.ns.ca/
enla/labstand/minwage.htm
http://canadaonline.about.com/library/bl/blminwage.htm

Province	General Wage	More Information
Alberta	$7.00	Alberta Human Resources and Employment
BC	$8.00	B.C. Ministry of Labour
Manitoba	$7.25	Manitoba Labour
New Brunswick	$6.30	Employment Standards
Newfoundland	$6.25	Department of Labour
NWT	$8.25	
Nova Scotia	$6.50	Department of Labour
Nunavut	$8.50	
Ontario	$7.45	Ministry of Labour
PEI	$6.80	Community and Cultural Affairs
Quebec	$7.60	Commission des normes du travail
Saskatchewan	$7.05	Saskatchewan Labour
Yukon	$7.20	

Note: See **Chapter 5** for information on **Credential Assessment.**

Note: Canada is a nation of many self-employed persons, so small businesses are prevalent.

Government Assistance:

http://www.jobsetc.ca/

Job Listing Websites:

http://www.theworkplace.ca/page.asp?sect=2

http://www.workopolis.com/content/aboutus

http://workdestinations.org/home.jsp?lang=en

http://company.monster.ca/

http://globalgateway.monster.ca/

http://www.bestjobsca.com/

http://www.hrdc-drhc.gc.ca/redirect_hr.html

http://www.jobs.com/

http://www.jobspress.com/

http://www.canadajobs.com

http://ca.hotjobs.yahoo.com

http://www.sjcjobs.com/default.asp

Company Directories:

http://www.strategis.gc.ca/sc_coinf/engdoc/homepage.html

Some Job Opportunities are currently available in:

- Financial services, IT[xxvi].
- Science.
- Healthcare.
- Construction.

See this site: http://www.immigration.ca/tempent-faq-faq.asp

Work in Canada Forum that may be helpful:

http://www.workincanada.net

List of Job Shortages in Some Provinces: (See # 5 in the link below)

http://www.canadaimmigrationvisa.com/oejs.html#hrdc

Labour Market Information:
http://www.labourmarketinformation.ca/

Employment Standards Act 2000:
http://192.75.156.68/DBLaws/Statutes/English/00e41_e.htm#P572_24537

Standard Hours, Wages, Vacations, Holidays: (Legal Text)
http://laws.justice.gc.ca/en/L-2/17658.html

Payroll Deductions Tables:
http://www.cra-arc.gc.ca/tax/business/topics/payroll/t4032jan05/menu-e.html

Public Holidays in Canada: (National and Provincial)
http://www.pch.gc.ca/progs/cpsc-ccsp/jfa-ha/index_e.cfm

(New Years' Day, Good Friday, Easter Monday, Victoria Day, Canada Day, Labour Day, Thanksgiving Day, Remembrance Day, Christmas Day, Boxing Day).

Media in Canada: (a few of the major ones)

http://www.cbc.ca/business/

http://www.canada.com/national/nationalpost/financialpost/index.html

http://www.theglobeandmail.com/business/

http://www.ctv.ca

34
Work Permits & Temporary Resident Visas

http://www.cic.gc.ca/english/pdf/kits/guides/5487E.PDF

http://www.cic.gc.ca/english/pdf/kits/forms/IMM5488E.PDF

http://www.hrsdc.gc.ca/en/epb/lmd/fw/tempoffers.shtml

http://careers-carrieres.nrc-
cnrc.gc.ca/Careers/career_main.nsf/pagee/newcomers.html

Over 90,000 workers enter Canada every year to work temporarily to help
Canadian employers overcome skill shortages. CIC and HRSDC work together to
ensure that these workers support growth in Canada and create more opportunities
for all Canadian job seekers[xxvii].

In order to work in Canada, in most cases you must have a valid work permit.
Before you apply for a work permit, you must be offered a job by a Canadian
employer and HRSDC must provide a LMO (Labour Market Opinion) or
"confirmation" of your job offer (some types of work are exempt). After HRSDC
confirms that a foreign national may fill the job, you then apply to CIC for your
work permit.

http://www.cic.gc.ca/english/applications/work.html

Jobs Exempt from a LMO from HRDC (Labour Market Opinion):
http://www.cic.gc.ca/english/work/exempt-2.html

Jobs Exempt from a Work Permit:
http://www.cic.gc.ca/english/work/exempt-1.html

Note: You cannot immigrate with a work permit. You would still need to apply
under one of the immigration classes such as the Skilled Worker Class. Bear in
mind too that it is best to apply for a Work Permit before applying for Permanent
Residency due to the problem of dual intent.

Countries Requiring a Visa to Visit Canada:
http://www.cic.gc.ca/english/visit/visas.html

Note: A US Citizen is not required to have a visa to visit Canada for a stay of up to 180 days. To enter Canada you should show a US passport or a birth certificate, although a passport is the preferred choice nowadays (This may be changing. See the Consular link below).

http://travel.state.gov/travel/cis_pa_tw/cis/cis_1082.html?css=print

Hiring Skilled Workers and Supporting their Permanent Residence:
http://www.hrsdc.gc.ca/en/epb/lmd/fw/supperimm.shtml

Entertainment & Film Jobs:
http://www.hrsdc.gc.ca/en/epb/lmd/fw/entertainment.shtml

Social Security Totalisation Agreement:

This agreement between the US and Canada provides that a US citizen working in Canada on a temporary assignment (of up to five years) for a US company is exempt from CPP (Canada Pension Plan) so long as he/she remains covered by US social security. To prove that you have coverage, a certificate must be obtained from the Social Security Administration. This agreement does not apply to US citizens employed by Canadian companies in Canada[xxviii].

Career Guides Available: (23 Countries including Canada and US)

http://www.goinglobal.com/default.asp

Work in Canada Forum that may be helpful:

http://www.workincanada.net/bbxc/viewforum.php?f=3

35
Using a Representative

A Representative can be an immigration consultant, lawyer, friend, family member, and so forth who conducts business with CIC and the Canada Border Services Agency (CBSA) on your behalf[xxix].

Canadian Society of Immigration Consultants[xxx]:

http://www.csic-scci.ca/home.html

In 2002, an advisory panel was created to identify various problems within the immigration consulting industry. As a result, the **Canadian Society of Immigration Consultants** was created, whose job it is to oversee the industry so that consumers are protected.

The consultants who are members of this society must demonstrate their knowledge of the industry, take an ethics test and must be of good character. Members must also carry Errors and Omissions Insurance, a minimum of $1 million. There are also Rules of Professional Conduct, which each member must abide by. The site also lists consultants who have been suspended, so you should check this out.

The need for regulation in this industry stems from many issues. There were no set standards for the levels of education, quality of service or professional accountability to offer services as a consultant in this field. Some applicants did not even know the difference between an immigration consultant and a lawyer. The result was that many consultants were being unscrupulous, saying they were experts but really having little or no training.

The Government of Canada amended the *Immigration and Refugee Protection Regulations* in April, 2004 stating that all practicing immigration consultants in Canada need to be members in good standing with either the Canadian Society of Immigration Consultants, a Canadian law society or the Chambre des notaries du Quebec in order to participate in new matters before CIC, the Immigration and Refugee Board (IRB) and the Canadian Border Services Agency (CBSA)[xxxi].

After April 13, 2008, paid representatives must be a member of one of the three organisations listed above.

Citizenship Immigration Canada (CIC):

If you hire a representative, you will need to complete the "Use of a Representative" Form IMM 5476, which authorizes CIC to release information to your representative.

Refer to the CIC website, "Instructions – Use of a Representative" (Form IMM 5561). CIC will not recommend a specific representative, nor vouch for their competence. If you hire a representative, it is entirely your choice and responsibility.

Suggestions – If Hiring a Consultant:

Contact the **Canadian Society of Immigration Consultants** (CSIC). They cannot recommend a specific consultant, but they can provide a list of members in good standing and a list of those who are not.

Verify the representative. See list at following site:
http://www.cic.gc.ca/english/department/consultants/verify-rep.html

- Ask the representative for references and proof of membership in the Canadian Society of Immigration Consultants.
- Discuss fees with the representative prior to signing a contract (a reasonable range is US$1,600 to $2,400).
- Choose a representative who fits your personality as this could be a long-term relationship.

Do I Need a Representative?

CIC does not require you to have a representative and they are not associated with any representatives. CIC treats every applicant equally. Hiring a representative does not give you special attention, faster processing or a more favourable outcome.

This decision must be based on your particular needs and financial resources. It is more economical to do it yourself if you have the time and patience to complete all the paperwork with attention to detail.

Where to File Complaints:

If you happen to hire an unscrupulous consultant and they are a member of the **Canadian Society of Immigration Consultants**, you may file a complaint with the society. If the representative does not belong to the society, you can file a complaint with the **Better Business Bureau** in the province or territory where the representative works.

Better Business Bureau:

http://www.canadiancouncilbbb.ca/

36
History of Americans in Canada

For more than a hundred years, Canada has been a safe haven for those seeking refuge. The following gives a synopsis of the history of Americans seeking refuge in Canada.

United Empire Loyalists (1776 – 1784):

The United Empire Loyalists were settlers who were loyal to the British cause in the American Revolution. They migrated from the Thirteen Colonies to the Maritimes of Canada. Some emigrated during the Revolution, but the greatest number left the colonies in 1783-84 after the Treaty of Paris failed to make adequate provision for the Loyalists. It is estimated that as many as 50,000 went to what are now the provinces of Nova Scotia and Quebec.

Since many settled north of the Bay of Fundy, this region was separated from Nova Scotia and organized as New Brunswick in 1784. Others went to the region north of the Great Lakes and the St. Lawrence River which in 1791 became what is now Ontario.

The Loyalists were strongest in the far southern colonies of Georgia and the Carolinas and also in New York and Pennsylvania. They came from every class and walk of life. They had little in common except their opposition to the American Revolution. The common thread that linked them was a distrust of too much democracy, which they believed resulted in "mob rule" and an accompanying breakdown of law and order. They believed that the British connection guaranteed them a more secure and prosperous life than republicanism would[xxxii].

Underground Railroad to Canada: (1810 – 1850) [xxxiii]

The Underground Railway helped American slaves escape captivity and provided them with a new home. As many as 50,000 – 100,000 African Americans found sanctuary in Canada during the early years when the USA still condoned the buying and selling of human beings. The majority came to Ontario and Nova Scotia, while some escaped to Vancouver Island, British Columbia. The network of sympathetic black and white abolitionists that assisted in the escapes along their secret routes became known as the Underground Railroad[xxxiv].

The Thirteenth Amendment to the US Constitution abolished slavery and was ratified by the required three-fourths of the States in 1865.

Vietnam War Resisters: (1964 – 1977)

The Vietnam War sparked another exodus, bringing many American war resisters north to Canada. Approximately 125,000 American war resisters came to Canada between 1964 and 1977.

In April, 1975, the war ended. Then in 1977, President Jimmy Carter issued an amnesty to all the draft dodgers. Sociologist John Hagen estimates that 50,000 draft dodgers settled in Canada becoming teachers, artists, musicians, journalists and writers[xxxv]. This was the largest political exodus in US history.

Summary:

It is interesting that there seems to be a historical trend of Americans seeking refuge in Canada from injustices in their own country. Canada prides itself on being a peaceful country with a real heart for human rights, even tracing right back to its early origins. Once again, in 2005, some American soldiers who resisted the war in Iraq looked north of the border for refuge. Since the US now has a voluntary military, however, the result may not be the same as in earlier wars.

Recent changes in Canadian laws are also now leading to more gays and lesbians coming to Canada, so that they can be afforded the right to be treated equal in their relationships. So the story continues but now it is for different reasons.

37

Exchange Rates – Getting the Best

http://www.escapeartist.com/currency/currency.htm
http://www.independenttraveler.com/resources/article.cfm?AID=44&category=8

Dos:

- Exchange large sums at one time.
- Ask for the Buy Rate when exchanging US dollars into foreign currency (sell rates are usually advertised).
- Ask for the "spot rate" at a bank if exchanging $5,000 or more.
- Compare at least three institutions, as rates vary widely. Banks and post offices usually have good rates.
- If you already deal with a brokerage firm, you can generally exchange money at no or very low commissions.
- Use a Mastercard or Visa issued by a bank that does not add a surcharge to foreign billings when traveling (see chart).

Don'ts:

- Do not use Canadian cash for the exchange. Cheques or traveller's cheques generally attract the best rates.
- Do not exchange money at airports or change bureaus. These have the highest fees.
- Amex and Diner's Club cards charge a slightly higher fee – 2%. If you use Amex cheques, however, you can get a lower fee.
- Do not use your credit card to get cash, as the rate is higher.
- If your bank doesn't offer no-fee withdrawals, you will pay up to $3 each time you use a foreign ATM.

ATM Locators:

Visa - http://visa.via.infonow.net/locator/global/jsp/SearchPage.jsp

Master Card - http://www.mastercard.com/atmlocator/index.jsp

Currency Conversion Online:

http://www.xe.com/ucc
http://www.bankofcanada.ca/en/rates/exchform.html

Foreign Exchange Brokers:	
Custom House Currency Exchange http://www.customhouse.com	A very good foreign exchange broker that is based in Victoria, BC Canada. They also have offices in the US, UK among other countries. 1 (800) 345-0007 (US & Canada)
Credit Card Companies:	
Capital One http://www.capitalone.com	Does not add a surcharge to foreign billings and offers a preferred exchange rate when you use their cards to purchase foreign goods charging only 1%.
MBNA http://www.mbna.com	Same as above.
Bank of Montreal http://www.bmo.com	Issues a US dollar Visa card, meaning you pay in US dollars.
Online Banking:	
Bank Direct http://www.bankdirect.com/	Same as above
Banks/Debit/ATM Cards:	
Bank of America http://www.bankofamerica.com http://www.atmmarketplace.com/news_story_10252.htm	A member of the Global ATM Alliance that offers reciprocal no-fee ATM use and no surcharge, so all you lose when exchanging money is the standard 1% fee. Global ATM Alliance Announcement.
Scotiabank (Canada) http://www.scotiabank.com	A member of the Global ATM Alliance that offers reciprocal no-fee ATM use and no surcharge.
Citibank http://www.citibank.com/us/index.htm	Another good bank with branches in many countries. They do not charge a fee or surcharge when exchanging money.

Government of Canada Websites

http://www.canada.gc.ca

Human Resources & Skills Development Canada

http://www.hrsdc.gc.ca

Social Development Canada

http://www.sdc.gc.ca

Canada Customs and Revenue Agency

http://www.ccra-adrc.gc.ca

Health Canada

http://www.hc-sc.gc.ca

Environment Canada

http://www.ec.gc.ca

Housing in Canada

http://www.cmhc-schl.gc.ca

Other Useful Sites for Maps:

http://www.mapquest.com

http://maps.google.com

Glossary

Admissible - means you are in good health, have no criminal record, are not a security risk to Canada and have not been charged with a criminal offense in Canada or abroad.

Alien – this term is used in some countries, notably the US, to designate non-citizens.

Arranged employment – a guaranteed job offer by a Canadian employer that has been validated by Human Resources Canada and that no suitably qualified Canadian or permanent resident is available to fill. This can include post-graduate work in Canada and NAFTA qualified persons.

Background check – a check that CIC conducts to determine if you have any arrests or convictions or represent a security risk to Canada.

Canadian citizen – a person who is Canadian by birth or who has applied for citizenship through Citizenship and Immigration Canada and has received a citizenship certificate. A permanent resident can apply for citizenship after living in Canada for three out of the last five years (or 1,095 days).

Common-law partner: two people in a genuine, committed relationship who have lived together for at least 12 months.

Conjugal partner – two people in a genuine, committed, interdependent relationship of some permanence. They must have been in the relationship for at least one year and have spent time together[xxxvi].

Convention refugee – someone with a well-founded fear of persecution for reasons of race, religion, nationality, membership in a particular social group or political opinion.

Dependent child – a son or daughter who is under 22 years of age and unmarried or not in a common-law relationship.

Deportation order – An order issued to a person who has violated the Immigration Act. It requires the person to leave Canada within a prescribed period and permits re-application for admission.

Designated occupation – An occupation in a locality or area in Canada designated by the Minister after consultation with the relevant provincial authority. This usually means that occupation is in short supply in that area.

Dual citizen – someone who is a citizen of two countries at the same time.

Dual intent – means that the individual has an intention to remain in Canada permanently, but is visiting in the interim and would depart if required to do so. Canada generally allows for such a possibility if the immigration official is satisfied.

Exclusion order – a removal order that bars the individual named in it from entering Canada for either one or two years, unless given written permission by CIC to return to Canada.

Excessive Demand – Refers to the significant burden placed on Canada's health or social services due to ongoing hospitalisation or medical, social or institutional care for physical or mental illnesses, or special education training. Persons may be denied admittance to Canada due to the high costs of care required.

Exit tax – a tax you pay when leaving Canada. This is not an additional tax, but a tax you would normally pay when disposing of an appreciated asset (see Chapter 17 on Cross-Border Tax Planning).

Foreign National – a person who is neither a Canadian citizen, nor a permanent resident. This includes a stateless person (according to Canada's *Immigration and Refugee Protection Act*).

Human Resources Canada (HRDC) - provides advice on local labour markets and is where you would apply for a Social Insurance Number (SIN).

Landed Immigrant – a person who applies to Canada for immigration and is accepted. This term is still used, but has officially been replaced by the term "permanent resident."

Landing – permission given to an individual that allows him or her to live as a permanent resident in Canada.

LMO (Labour Market Opinion) – An HRSDC confirmation is the opinion provided by Human Resources and Skills Development Canada (HRSDC) to the CIC officer that enables them to determine whether the employment of the foreign worker is likely to have a positive or negative impact on the labour market in Canada. An HRSDC confirmation may be required in order for a work permit to be issued

National Occupational Classification (NOC) – a classification system for jobs in Canada. A number is assigned to each classification, and then a more detailed description is given of that classification. A person immigrating under the Skilled Worker Class should be qualified in one of these areas.

Permanent Resident (formerly Landed Immigrant) – a person who has been granted permanent resident status in Canada. The person may have come to Canada as an immigrant or as a refugee. Permanent residents who become

Canadian citizens are no longer permanent residents. You can change employers, relocate and sponsor family members. If you came to Canada as a Skilled Worker, you can even stay in Canada if you lose your job.

Person without status/Undocumented – a person who has not been granted permission to stay in the country, or has overstayed their visa. The term can cover a person who falls between the cracks of the system, such as a refugee claimant who is refused refugee status but not removed from Canada because of a situation of generalised risk in their country of origin. The term "undocumented" can be confusing because it is also used in Canada to refer to refugees who lack identity documents from their country of origin.

Principal applicant – The person who completes the application.

Protected person – according to the *Immigration and Refugee Protection Act*, a protected person is someone who has been determined by Canada to be either a Convention Refugee or a person in need of protection (that is, a person who may not meet the definition of a Convention Refugee but is in a refugee-like situation, who under Canadian law is defined as deserving protection (if, for example, they are in danger of being tortured or something similar).

Refugee – a person who is forced to flee their country for fear of persecution.

Refugee protection claimant – a person who requests refugee protection status, either from abroad or from within Canada. If their claim is accepted, they become a protected person and may become a permanent resident of Canada.

Removal order – an order issued by the Immigration and Refugee Board or an immigration officer that requires the named person to leave the country within a specified time. There are three types of removal orders: an exclusion order, a departure order and a deportation order.

Representative – an immigration consultant, lawyer, friend, family member, or other who conducts business with CIC and the Canada Border Services Agency (CBSA) on your behalf.

Sponsor – a group, corporation, unincorporated organisation or association that sponsors a successful refugee claimant or a person in a similar circumstance. A sponsor can also be a Canadian citizen or permanent resident who is at least 18 years of age, resides in Canada and has filed a sponsorship application in respect of a member of the Family Class or the Spouse and Common-Law Partner In Canada Class.

Study permit – a document issued by a visa or immigration officer authorising a foreign national to study in Canada.

Temporary Resident – a temporary resident is a person who resides in Canada lawfully for a temporary purpose. Temporary residents include students, foreign workers and visitors such as tourists.

Visitor record – The official document that allows a visitor to extend his/her stay in Canada. It is only issued by an immigration officer in Canada and is only valid for a specified length of time.

Visitor status – Also called "valid status" and refers to the period of time a visitor has permission to be in Canada temporarily.

Visitor's visa – A document issued by a visa officer and placed in the passport of an authorised visitor to Canada. It is an official way of showing that the person has met the requirements for admission to Canada as a visitor.

Work permit – a document that authorises a foreign national to work in Canada.

Index

2

Map of Canada

2http://listingsca.com/maps.asp

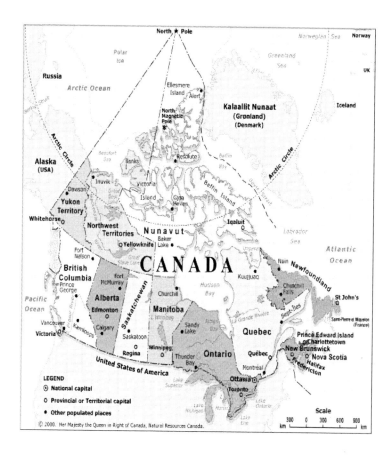

Endnotes

[i] http://www.members.shaw.ca/kcic1/canada.html

[ii] http://www.gommage.com/peace.html

[iii] http://canada.justice.gc.ca/en/news/fs/2003/doc_30898.html

[iv] http://hdr.undp.org/statistics/data/cty/cty_f_CAN.html

[v] http://hdr.undp.org/statistics/data/cty/cty_f_USA.html

[vi] http://www.cic.gc.ca/english/pdf/pub/look.pdf "A Look at Canada"

[vii] http://www12.statcan.ca/english/census01/products/standard/popdwell/Table-PR.cfm

[viii] http://www.gg.ca/menu_e.asp

[ix] http://www.cic.gc.ca/english/pdf/pub/look.pdf

[x] http://www.cic.gc.ca/english/pdf/kits/guides/5289E.PDF   See pg 3.
[xi] http://www.richw.org/dualcit/faq.html#possible

[xii] "The Border Guide", by Robert Keats, 2004 pg 155.
http://www.keatsconnelly.com/pages/f_border_guide.htm
[xiii] "The Border Guide", by Robert Keats, 2004 pg 65
[xiv] http://bearclawtours.com/usa.htm

[xv] "The Border Guide", by Robert Keats, 2004 pg 175
[xvi] Keats, Robert, "The Border Guide" pg 57
[xvii] Keats, Robert, "The Border Guide" pg 62
[xviii] Keats, Robert pg 11 "Border Guide"
[xix] Keats, Robert "The Border Guide" pg 211
[xx] Keats, Robert "The Border Guide" pg 13
[xxi] Keats, Robert "The Border Guide" pg 42
[xxii] Keats, Robert "The Border Guide" 7th edition pg 118 & 240
[xxiii] http://laws.justice.gc.ca/en/C-6/

[xxiv] http://www.hrsdc.gc.ca/en/epb/lmd/fw/supperimm.shtml

[xxv] http://www.cic.gc.ca/english/work/exempt-2.html

[xxvi] http://www.hrsdc.gc.ca/en/epb/lmd/fw/infotech.shtml

[xxvii] http://www.cic.gc.ca/english/work/index.html

4

[xxviii] Mark Serbinski, "Taxation of US Citizens Living and/or Working in Canada", 8.
http://www.serbinski.com

[xxix] http://www.cic.gc.ca/english/applications/representative.html

[xxx] http://www.csic-scci.ca/indexE.html

[xxxi] http://www.csic-scci.ca/history.html

[xxxii] http://www.uelac.org/whatis.html

[xxxiii] http://www.democracynow.org/article.pl?sid=04/10/15/157205

[xxxiv] http://www.pc.gc.ca/canada/proj/cfc-ugrr/index_E.asp

[xxxv] http://en.wikipedia.org/wiki/Draft-dodger

[xxxvi] LEGIT Vancouver http://www.legit.ca/contact.html